The Struggle is Real

But So is God

Misty Phillip

By His Grace

ISBN - 0578493799

Dedication

When I set out to write a Bible study, I truly had no idea what I was getting myself into. What you now hold in your hands is possible only by the amazing grace of Jesus Christ, and the love and support of my friends and family.

A special thank you to Pastor David Fleming and life group leader Mark Lanier of Champion Forest Baptist Church, as well as countless other mentors and friends who prayed and spoke into this study, including Kristin, Ann and the Bible Babes, and my Mastermind friends.

To my family:
This study would never have been written without you. Peter, Jacob, Jane, Connor, and Ian, you are my heartbeat.

Thanks for believing in me and helping me turn my dream into a reality.

To Christ alone be the glory!

Table of Contents

Welcome to The Struggle Is Real Bible Study!

Hey friend, have you ever heard the expression, "the struggle is real"? We use that phrase in jest to talk about having a bad hair day, and we chuckle about it, but sometimes the struggles in life are real and they are not a joking matter.

I have good news for you: **the struggle is real, but so is God!** Jesus Christ came that we might have a hope and a future. With Jesus, Scripture, and the Holy Spirit, we need not worry about our present troubles because, through Jesus, we have already overcome!

The Bible is filled with stories of imperfect men and women who faced all sorts of obstacles and challenges in their lives. Each of their lives was touched by the grace of a loving Father who continues to redeem all things to himself through Christ. I have heard it said that history is His-Story. It is a beautiful story of redemption from the beginning until now.

My life has been filled with many struggles and challenges, some of my own making, others as a result of living in a fallen world. Some suffering I have endured because the Lord has allowed things to happen in my life for His good and His glory. Through it all, the Lord has taught me the importance of living in victory, and it is my joy to walk you through what He has shown me.

Friend, we all have hard things that we go through. My trials may not look like your trials because difficulties come in all shapes and sizes. But what I do know for sure is that, no matter what you are facing right now, God is there to see you through to the end. You are an overcomer, and God wants you to live in victory!

The theme of overcoming is magnificently woven throughout the Bible. God is not silent on the matter. In this study, we will delve into the Word of God to see what scripture has to say about living a victorious life and follow the theme of overcoming throughout the Bible. We will examine it in light of the Holy Spirit's wisdom and draw on the promises and good news of scripture. We will also consult biblical commentaries, along with Greek and Hebrew word studies, to enhance our understanding. At the conclusion of each day, a section of practical application will help us apply what we've learned.

God has given us the lives of the men and women of both the Old and New Testaments to serve as examples of how we should live. The Bible is the word of God, and it is a beautiful love letter from the Lord to his children. Through the promises of scripture, we have everything we need to overcome any problem, challenge, or stressful situation we face in our lives.

We see this clearly illustrated in 2 Peter:

> His divine power has granted to us all things that pertain to life and godliness, through the knowledge of him who called us to his own glory and excellence, by which he has granted to us his precious and very great promises, so that through them you may become partakers of the divine nature, having escaped from the corruption that is in the world because of sinful desire.
> (2 Peter 1:3-5 English Standard Version, emphasis added)

There are great promises for those who put their faith and trust in Jesus Christ as their Lord and Savior. When we believe in Him, God gives us His divine power through Christ. It is the same power that raised Jesus from the grave! By knowing Him, by spending time reading, studying, and memorizing His word, and through prayer to Him, we have everything we need to live in victory.

What to Expect

The primary Bible used for this study is the English Standard Version (ESV), unless otherwise noted. We will look at other translations throughout the study, and those verses will be provided with the text. Please use the Bible translation that you are most comfortable using.

This study is broken into daily assignments, five days a week. The focus of the study is to draw you closer to Jesus. It can be done individually, in a group session with a church, or by simply grabbing a few friends and going through the study together. The benefit of having a group is to keep each other accountable and pray for one another. We are made for community.

Wherever you are in your walk with the Lord, it is my prayer that He uses this study to draw you closer to Him. Grab your Bible and a pen, and find a comfortable, quiet, cozy spot. Let's learn what it means to be an overcomer by becoming intimately acquainted with the Overcomer Himself, Jesus Christ.

enjoy

why I wrote this study

I met Jesus when I was six years old at Vacation Bible School. For many years, He was my acquaintance. I understood who Jesus was but He didn't play a big role in my life. I had a head knowledge of Jesus, but not a heart knowledge. I recognized Jesus as my Savior, but He wasn't Lord over my life." I believed He died for me, but I didn't understand what that meant.

In junior high school, my brother died, and my life turned into a train wreck as I began looking for anything I could find to ease the pain. Everything changed when I went to college and had a life-altering encounter with Jesus Christ, and I have never been the same!

In my mid-twenties, I did my first Bible study and was hooked. I fell head-over-heels in love with Jesus and his word. Studying the Bible became my lifeline through illness, pain, grief, the loss of babies and parents, the difficulties of raising a special needs child, homeschooling, and the challenges of life.

Even though I had a relationship with Jesus Christ, I spent many of those years living a defeated life because of my circumstances. For many years my life was really hard, and to make matters worse I held on to hurt and shame from my past instead of activating scripture in my life and claiming the promises available to me in the Bible.

I wrote The Struggle is Real: But So Is God Bible study because I want you to know my friend Jesus the way I do. I want you to lay claim to the promises available to you in scripture so that you can walk in the victorious freedom of Christ.

The Struggles in life are indeed real, but my friend, so is God. May you experience just how real He is and know He is right there with you in the middle of it all. He loves and cares for you greatly, and His Grace is enough to see you through.

Much Love,

Misty Phillip

Week 1

WHAT DOES IT MEAN TO OVERCOME?

the overcoming life

DAY 1

Trials should not surprise us or cause us to doubt God's faithfulness. Rather, we should actually be glad for them. God sends trials to strengthen our trust in him so that our faith will not fail. Our trials keep us trusting; they burn away our self-confidence and drive us to our Savior. –Edmund Clowney[1]

As the thought of what it means to overcome began swirling in my head, I visited my local theological library. I began with a simple search at the library for the word "overcoming." Here are a few of the titles my search returned:

Overcoming Frustration and Anger
Overcoming Depression
Overcoming the Adversary
Overcoming Jealousy and Possessiveness
Overcoming Worry and Fear
Overcoming Sin and Temptation

You can find a book to overcome almost anything, from overcoming addiction to overcoming shyness. In total, my search at the library returned a list of 50 books about overcoming various challenges, but there are hundreds more. What I noticed is that all of the books that surfaced in the search were about overcoming specific things, like how to overcome frustration, anger, worry, fear, sin, or depression. There were so many books about overcoming!

So why would I want to write another book on the topic? Because I want to show you that the Bible is the only thing you need. The Bible is God's love letter to us. It is the guidebook for our lives and contains everything we need to live an abundant, victorious life.

The Meaning of Overcomer

What does being an overcomer mean to you? What image does that word evoke? Does the word "overcomer" make you think of Sylvester Stallone in the movie *Rocky*? Maybe if you listen to contemporary Christian music, hearing the word "overcomer" makes you think about Mandisa belting out the words, "You're an overcomer!"

Take a moment to think about what it means to be an overcomer and use the space below to write your answer.

_____

_____

According to the *Cambridge Dictionary*, the word "overcome" is a verb that means, "to defeat or succeed in controlling or dealing with something. To overcome difficulties, obstacles, problems, resistance." The usage example the dictionary provides is, "I believe that we will overcome in the end."[2]

Interestingly, *Merriam-Webster* defines "overcome" in a slightly different way: "to get the better of: surmount—overcome difficulties." The example of usage of the word in *Merriam-Webster Dictionary* is, "They overcame the enemy."[3]

Digging Deeper

For further understanding, let's look to the original language. The New Testament was written in Koine Greek, a beautiful and amazingly descriptive language. If you were to look up the word for "overcomer" in Greek, according to *Strong's Concordance*, the word is νικάω (nikáō), which means "to conquer or prevail."[4]

It is used many times throughout the New Testament. The verb *nikáō* comes from *níkē*, which means "victory." Nike . . . is that a familiar word? I live in a house full of boys, and my boys love all things Nike! Nike's very slogan, "Just do it," evokes victory. To overcome means to have victory. According to New Testament Greek Scholar Kenneth Wuest, *nikáō* means, "to conquer, to carry off the victory, come off victorious."[5]

Craig R. Koester, in his book *Revelation, A New Translation with Introduction and Commentary*, describes overcoming this way: "To those who conquer. The verb *nikan* means conquest and victory."[6] A verb is an action word, which implies that we are doing something. As a Christian, we are in a battle, and that is the real struggle we all face daily. But the good news is that in Christ we are triumphant. #JesusWins

Have you ever thought of your Christian life as a battle?

_____

_____

When you think of a warrior, what images does that evoke?

_____

_____

Overcoming Trials

Although the world is full of suffering, it is also full of overcoming it. –Helen Keller[7]

We all experience challenges in life. I have experienced firsthand a life marred by difficulty and strife, but I also know the challenges I have faced have made me into the woman I am today. It is the same for you, friend. We want to move through pain as quickly as possible, but anguish drives us to our knees and brings us closer to the lover of our souls. The challenges that you have faced in the past, as well as the ones you may be struggling with today, are the very things that God is using to transform you into the image of who you were made to be.

When Tragedy Strikes

A few years ago, I broke both of my arms at the same time and dislocated my wrist. I was bicycling with my boys, and I wasn't wearing a helmet. I know—you should always wear a helmet! But it was hot that day, and besides, I grew up riding a bike without wearing a helmet. Not wearing one was my first mistake that day. The second mistake was thinking that I was clever by using Velcro to attach my phone to the handlebars so I could track my progress and change my music.

The third mistake happened when my phone began to slip out of place and jerked my earbuds out of my ears. I instinctively grabbed the left brake to stop so that my headphones wouldn't get caught in the wheels when, all of a sudden, I came to a screeching halt and catapulted over my handlebars. As I flew through the air, I put my arms out in front of me to protect my head, and that is when I snapped both of my arms.

It took me a year to recover, a process that included one surgery, three plates and twenty screws, two removable casts, six months of physical therapy, and three huge scars on my arms. For months, I couldn't do anything for myself. I couldn't feed myself, brush my hair or my teeth, put makeup on, or dress myself. I had to rely on my husband and boys to do everything.

As terrible and traumatic as it was to have two broken arms, I was comforted when I realized that one of the things I could still do was pray. Unable to control what was happening all around me, the thing that got me through those days of excruciating pain and helplessness was my constant communication with the Lord. As awful as that experience was, God used it in a powerful way to show me how much He loved and cared for me.
I don't know what difficult situation you may be facing today, friend, but I do know that you have a loving Heavenly Father that sees you in the midst of your affliction. Nothing escapes his watchful eye. He loves and cares for you dearly.

Setting the Stage

Let's begin by looking at a few fundamental truths from the word of God as a foundation to build this study upon. Look up the following verses and then write out your answers to the questions that follow.

Take a quick look at John 1:1-5. What do we learn about Jesus? Jot down your initial thoughts.
_____
_____

According to 2 Timothy 3:16, how can I know that the Bible pertains to me?
_____
_____

What is the promise we can hold on to in Philippians 1:6?
_____
_____

What can we learn from Galatians 6:9?
_____
_____

What assurances does God give us in Psalm 46:1?
_____
_____

These verses illustrate how, from the foundation of the universe, Jesus was with God and is God. He is the word of God who became flesh and dwelt among us. All things were made through Him, and in Him there is light. He himself is the light of the world, the bright, shining beacon of hope that overcomes the darkness of this world.

The whole counsel of the Bible is profitable to teach, train, and correct us so that it may equip us for the work God has for us. The breath of God is infused into scripture, and the word of God teaches us what is true. It corrects us when we are wrong and teaches us to do what is right. His word is true, and if we study it, we will be changed.

Take a look at Isaiah 55:10-11 (ESV):

> For as the rain and the snow come down from heaven and do not return there but water the earth, making it bring forth and sprout, giving seed to the sower and bread to the eater, so shall my word be that goes out from my mouth; it shall not return to me empty, but it shall accomplish that which I purpose, and shall succeed in the thing for which I sent it.

God's word does not come back void and it shall not return to us empty. It will accomplish His purpose in my life and in yours. Something happens every time you pick up the word of God and read it. If you press in to His word, you will be changed!

What does Proverbs 30:5 say about the word of God?

_____

_____

What does 2 Samuel 22:31 say about every word of the Lord?

_____

_____

Aren't you glad to know that every word of God spoken proves true and will not return void? I love what the New International Version says in Proverbs 30:5, "Every word of God is flawless." The Message frames it in a slightly different way: "every promise of God proves true; He protects everyone who runs to Him for help." His word is trustworthy, and we can depend on the promises contained in it. As several translations of 2 Samuel 22:31 say, "His way is perfect."

I am so thankful that God's way is perfect. As we study His word, it accomplishes in us God's purposes. It changes us from the inside out.

Prayer

Heavenly Father, thank you so much for Your Son, Jesus Christ, the King of Kings. He is everything. He is the word made flesh in John 1—fully man and fully God, yet without sin. He dwelled among us, suffered for our sins, died, was buried and resurrected, and now lives and reigns on high, seated at Your right hand.

Thank You for Your word and the promises it contains for our lives. Thank You that through Your divine power You have given us everything we need to live a godly life. Help us to know Your Word, to grow closer in relationship to You each day through Jesus, and to hold on to Your promises even in our darkest hours. We live in a fallen creation and uncertain times.

None of what is going on in our world today takes You by surprise, however. Lord, help us to live each day as overcomers, because without you, Lord, we are nothing. In the precious name of Jesus, I pray. Amen.

We need to know, without a shadow of a doubt, that the one who began a good work in us is faithful to complete it. We can remind ourselves of what God says about us by making His word personal and by declaring His truths back to ourselves. As Proverbs 18:21 teaches us, "Death and life are in the power of the tongue, and those who love it will eat its fruits." We will proclaim truth to ourselves throughout the study by taking key verses and ideas grounded in scripture and turning them into declarations.

A declaration makes God's Word personal and applicable to your life. I have friends that call it preaching to themselves. Whatever you call it, it is simply speaking truths aloud over yourself for the purpose of making the scripture come alive. It is both a powerful and practical tool we can use to make God's truths personal and applicable.

Declarations

God, You are faithful to do what only You can do in our lives. My responsibility is to yield to You. I trust You, Lord, because You are faithful.

I must not get tired of doing good, because I will reap a harvest if I don't quit.

God, You are my refuge and my strength. You are my help when I am in trouble. You are near me, Lord. All I have to do is call upon Your name and You will come to my rescue.

Overcoming in Your Life

Share your heart with your Heavenly Father. Let Him know about any struggles you have, burdens you are carrying, or challenges you are currently facing.

_____
_____

God wants to help us in our time of need and heal our brokenness. Do you need to forgive someone or deal with a past hurt? Forgive yourself for a past mistake? What is holding you back from walking in victory?

_____
_____

Are you plagued by worry, fear, anger, sin, or depression? Nothing is too hard for God. Share your struggles with Him and allow Him to begin healing the brokenness.

_____
_____
_____
_____

Good job today, friend! I am so excited to be on this journey with you and look forward to what the Lord has in store for you in the days and weeks ahead.

DAY 2

I have not departed from the commands of his lips; I have treasured the words of his mouth more than my daily bread. —Job 23:12 (NIV)

We all experience difficulties. Bad things happen, and people disappoint us. Sometimes people in our lives irritate or rub us the wrong way. They offend us, hurt our feelings, or may even cause us physical harm. If we are alive and breathing on planet earth, then trouble will find its way to us. We all have days when things don't go our way—a toilet overflows, a fender-bender happens while coming home from the grocery store, or any number of calamities occur that seek to steal our joy.

But when the bad days we experience become prolonged periods of adversity or suffering, we need endurance. I don't know what trial you are facing; maybe it is an illness, a divorce, a job loss, or perhaps a struggle with depression. In seasons of difficulty, life can seem desperately overwhelming! This is why it is important to look beyond ourselves and our circumstances for help.

Mom's Health Struggles

For decades, my Mom struggled with chronic health issues. They started the year I was born, when she was diagnosed with rheumatoid arthritis, and progressed as the years went on. By the time I was grown and had a family of my own, she was continuously in and out of the hospital. Suffering from the effects of an aortic aneurysm, her symptoms were complicated by emphysema, pneumonia, and lung cancer, which eventually led to a stroke. I watched my Mom's health deteriorate over the years until she was a shell of the woman of my youth. I stood by her side helplessly as disease ravaged her body. Watching a loved one suffer is anguishing when there is nothing that you can do to improve their health.

Throughout my Mom's illness, I pored over my Bible, and it was my lifeline of hope on dark days. Clinging to the promises of scripture increased my faith and helped me press on when her prognosis seemed grim. The good news for you is that those very same promises that helped to carry me through are also available to you, my friend.

A Salve to Our Weary Souls

God's word is a salve to our weary souls. I love what the apostle Paul says in Romans 8:18. What does Paul say about our current suffering in light of eternity?

_____

_____

Nothing we experience on this earth can compare to the glory that awaits us when we meet our Heavenly Father face-to-face. Even our deepest suffering is temporary in light of eternity. The New Living Translation says it this way, "Yet what we suffer now is nothing compared to the glory he will reveal to us later."

The apostle Paul was a man well-acquainted with suffering. Yet he knew that nothing he experienced here on earth compared to what lay before him in heaven.

In 2 Corinthians 4:8-9, he says, "We are afflicted in every way," but not what?

_____

_____

Paul faced many afflictions as a servant of Jesus Christ, but he did not lose heart. Paul knew that regardless of what happened to him on earth, it was temporary, and nothing could compare to the glory awaiting him in heaven. Affliction comes in many forms and presses on us from many directions, but Paul's words remind us not to despair.

Read 2 Corinthians 4:16-18:

> So do not lose heart. Though our outer self is wasting away, our inner self is being renewed day by day. For this light momentary affliction is preparing for us an eternal weight of glory beyond all comparison, as we look not to the things that are seen but to the things that are unseen. For the things that are seen are transient, but the things that are unseen are eternal. (ESV)

No matter what happens to us today, we can take comfort in knowing that the suffering we experience cannot defeat us. Even if our external person is being destroyed, what waits for us ahead in eternity is more glorious than we can ever imagine! Even the best day on earth pales in comparison to God's eternal glory.

What comfort do these verses provide?

_____

_____

Digging Deeper

Adam Clarke's commentary has this to say about these verses:

> But though our outward man—That is, our body—that part of us that can be seen, heard, and felt, perish—be slowly consumed by continual trials and afflictions, and be martyred at last . . . Yet the inward man—Our soul—that which cannot be felt or seen by others, is renewed—is revived, and receives a daily increase of light and life from God, so that we grow more holy, more happy, and more meet for glory every day.8

Oh, dear friend, aren't you glad that even though our external body may be fading away, our inward soul is renewed and revived?

Purpose

Let's conclude our lesson by looking at one final verse, Ephesians 2:10: "For we are his workmanship, created in Christ Jesus for good works, which God prepared beforehand, that we should walk in them" (ESV).

That same verse in the NIV says, "for we are God's handiwork," while the NLT says, "for we are God's masterpiece."

Have you ever considered that you are a masterpiece, a handiwork created by a loving Creator to carry out good things here and now?

_____

_____

God has kingdom work for each of us to do. We are all here for a purpose. Take some time to ponder the good works that God has prepared for you to walk in. Allow His word to be your guide. God has a plan for your life, and it is a good one. Trust Him with your fears and your pain.

Declarations

The problems and struggles of this world are temporary.

Nothing compares to the glory that awaits me!

I will not lose heart; I will keep the faith.

Though my body is wasting away, I know my soul is being renewed every day.

The challenges I face are helping me become more like Christ.

I will have faith and trust in the unseen hand of the Lord, who sees all.

Even though it feels like trouble surrounds me and I am pressed on every side, I will not despair. No matter what comes against me, I will remember the following: *I may suffer, but I am not crushed, I am not destroyed, and I am not abandoned.*

I may be persecuted but I am not forsaken. God loves me, and He wants good for me.

Overcoming in Your Life

At the most difficult times in my life, poring over the word of God and memorizing scripture brought me comfort. How has the word of God been a salve for your soul in this season of life?

_____

_____

Take a few moments to reflect upon all that the Lord is doing your life. Is there anything you need to surrender or submit to the Lord? Ask Him now.

_____

_____

Pray and ask God to reveal His will concerning the good works he has for you. Are you walking in those works now? Is anything hindering you from accomplishing them?

_____

_____

What would complete surrender look like in your life?

_____

_____

No matter what trials you are experiencing today, you do not need to lose heart. Remember that they are temporary and pale in comparison to what lies before you. Press on, friend, press on. There are brighter days ahead.

ready for battle?

DAY 3

The Christian life is a conflict and warfare, and the quicker we find it out, the better. –D.L. Moody[9]

Ready to dig into God's word today? From our Greek definitions, we have learned that we are in a battle. Now that we know that there is a battle and that we are in it, let's examine a few questions and consult the Bible for answers.

The Enemy

Who is our fight against? Why are we in a battle? What started this fight? When did it all begin? Keep these questions in the forefront of your mind as we go to the beginning of the Bible for some answers. Even if you are familiar with this story, don't glaze over it. Ask God to open the eyes of your heart and see the passage with fresh eyes.

The Fall in the Garden

Read Genesis 3:1-15, provided below. Here we read all about the fall of man in the Garden of Eden:

> Now the serpent was more crafty than any other beast of the field that the Lord God had made. He said to the woman, "Did God actually say, 'You shall not eat of any tree in the garden'?"
>
> The woman said to the serpent, "We may eat of the fruit of the trees in the garden, but God said, You shall not eat of the fruit of the tree that is in the midst of the garden, neither shall you touch it, lest you die.' "
>
> But the serpent said to the woman, "You will not surely die. For God knows that when you eat of it your eyes will be opened, and you will be like God, knowing good and evil."
>
> So when the woman saw that the tree was good for food, and that it was a delight to the eyes, and that the tree was to be desired to make one wise, she took of its fruit and ate, and she also gave some to her husband who was with her, and he ate.
>
> Then the eyes of both were opened, and they knew that they were naked. And they sewed fig leaves together and made themselves loincloths.

And they heard the sound of the Lord God walking in the garden in the cool of the day, and the man and his wife hid from the presence of the Lord God among the trees of paradise. But the Lord God called to the man and said to him, "Where are you?" And he said, "I heard the sound of you in the garden, and I was afraid, because I was naked, and I hid myself."

He said, "Who told you that you were naked? Have you eaten of the tree of which I commanded you not to eat?" The man said, "The woman whom you gave to be with me, she gave me fruit of the tree, and I ate." Then the Lord God said to the woman, "What is this that you have done?"

The woman said, "The serpent deceived me, and I ate." The Lord God said to the serpent, "Because you have done this, cursed are you above all livestock and above all beasts of the field; on your belly, you shall go, and dust you shall eat all the days of your life.

I will put enmity between you and the woman, and between your offering and her offspring; he shall bruise your head, and you shall bruise his heel. (Genesis 3:1-15 ESV)

What question did the serpent ask Eve?

_____

_____

The Question

Adam and Eve lived in a beautifully lush garden paradise and did not have a care in the world. They had direct access to God until sin entered the world, when the serpent (who we later find out is Satan) questions God's command. The serpent's question to Eve is the same one he uses today to entice people to sin. His question—*did God really say*—fuels our doubts about what we know is true of God and His nature. The war that we find ourselves in today is part of the battle that has raged ever since Satan rebelled against God and brought humankind into his schemes.

Because of their sin and rebellion in the Garden, God judged Adam and Eve by placing a curse on them and their offspring. We call this "the fall" because Adam and Eve fell from God's grace. Through their disobedience, the curse of sin entered the world and brought both physical and spiritual death, thus causing a separation between God and man.

Take note here that "the serpent was more crafty than any other beast of the field." The word for crafty in the Hebrew, *arum*, means subtle, sly, and cunning. Our enemy is deceptive and crafty.

Read Genesis 1:28.

What did Adam and Eve have dominion over?

_____

_____

Adam and Eve were to have dominion over all the earth, and they were to subdue it. The word "subdue" in Hebrew is *Kabash*, and it means to bring people or a land into subjection so that it will yield service to the one subduing it. [10] They were given the whole earth to develop into something useful and productive. They had rule over every living thing. Adam and Eve had dominion over all of the animals, including the serpents. They ruled over all of creation, but they did not exercise their dominion, and were deceived by the enemy. The enemy, disguised as a serpent, approached Eve in a subtle, shrewd, and cunning way.

The snake questioned Eve, "Did God really say?"

Can you just imagine the rest of the conversation? "God didn't really mean what He said, did He? Are you sure that is what He said?"

The serpent questioned God's goodness. He questioned morality and challenged God's law. Satan led Adam and Eve to doubt God's words. Instead, Satan persuaded them to trust their own ability to discern good and evil.

Satan's deception is even more poignant when you consider that he himself was once an angel who rebelled against God and became evil. Let's see what else we can learn by looking at the fall of angels and how that event influenced what happened later in the Garden of Eden.

Fall of Angels

There are two passages in the Old Testament that reveal a lot about our enemy, Satan. Read Isaiah 14:12-15 and Ezekiel 28:11-18.

> How you are fallen from heaven, O Day Star, son of Dawn!
> How you are cut down to the ground, you who laid the nations low!
> You said in your heart, 'I will ascend to heaven; above the stars of God
> I will set my throne on high; I will sit on the mount of assembly
> in the far reaches of the north; I will ascend above the heights of the clouds;
> I will make myself like the Most High.' But you are brought down to Sheol, to the
> far reaches of the pit. (Isaiah 14:12-15 ESV)

In Ezekiel 28, we see the King of Tyre and Babylon fall because of pride, arrogance, and rebellion. Satan's fall from heaven is seen symbolically in these passages. Verse 14 says, "I will ascend above the heights of the clouds; I will make myself like the Most High."

In 2 Peter 2:4, what is the punishment for angels who sinned?

_____

_____

Pride, Arrogance, and Rebellion

In Satan's pride and arrogance, he desired to be like God. He coveted the worship that only God deserves. God alone is worthy to be praised!

Satan's downfall was his pride, arrogance, and rebellion. I'm very familiar with these attributes! I wrestle with them, too. They are the same characteristics that lead us to sin and cause us to be tripped up in our Christian walk. To get a better picture of what these ideas entail, let's look at *Merriam-Webster's* simple definitions of the following words:

> Pride: "a feeling that you respect yourself and deserve to be respected by other people a feeling that you are more important or better than other people."11

> Arrogance: "an insulting way of thinking or behaving that comes from believing that you are better, smarter, or more important than other people."12

> Rebellion: "open opposition toward a person or group in authority."13

As our definitions illustrate, Satan wants to be worshipped. He thinks he deserves the respect that is only due to God. He considers himself better and more important than others. Because of these characteristics, he remains openly opposed to God.

Declarations

Lord, help me to not be deceived by the enemy.

The enemy of my soul is a fallen angel and a defeated foe.

Lord, you alone deserve to be praised!

Overcoming in Your Life

How has the enemy tried to deceive you in the past?

_____

_____

Is there anything other than God that seeks first place in your life?

_____

_____

God alone is worthy of our praise. Take a moment to praise Him, for He is worthy! Write out an offering of praise to the Lord.

_____

_____

_____

_____

_____

_____

_____

_____

spiritual battle with our enemy

DAY 4

Evil is real–and powerful. It has to be fought, not explained away, not fled. And God is against evil all the way. So each of us has to decide where we stand, how we're going to live our lives. –Catherine Marshall[14]

Catherine Marshall does not mince words. This is a woman who understands that we are in a war and knows that we must decide what side we are on.

There is a cosmic battle that began in the Garden of Eden, and we are participants in this battle. We must be aware that we are in a war and have a very real enemy. Although there is a spiritual battle playing out in the heavenly realms, we also feel the effects of that battle here on earth. The battlefield is in our mind, and the battle wages war in our flesh.

I love the way Tony Evans describes this in his book, *Victory in Spiritual Warfare*:

> Spiritual warfare is the cosmic conflict waged in the invisible, spiritual realm but simultaneously fleshed out in the visible, physical realm. To put it another way, the root of the war is something you cannot see, but the effects of the war are clearly seen and felt. This is because everything physical is either influenced or caused by something spiritual.[15]

We may not feel like we live in a war zone, but if we look closely at the world around us, we will notice how the effects of good versus evil play out in front of our eyes. Our enemy is not always visible, but he is always present. We must remain on guard in the fight for our hearts and lives.

Battling Through Grief

The first spiritual battle I was aware of happened when I was twelve, when my brother died. The enemy whispered lies to me. He tried to convince me that a good and loving God that was trustworthy wouldn't have taken my brother from me.

The enemy's plan was to destroy my family, and he did his best to try and tear our family apart. My Mom sank into a deep, dark depression and cried all the time. She was angry with my Dad, and she was angry at God. She lashed out in anger and took my brother's death out on him. This, in turn, drove my Dad away from us as he tried to keep the peace.

The Enemy is a Thief and a Liar

What does John 10:10 say?

_____

Our enemy, the devil, is an adversary who comes to steal, kill, and destroy. He wants to devour us. He is a thief bent on our destruction. He wants to steal our joy—our love for one another—by destroying us, our families, our relationships, and anything that brings glory to the Lord. We need to be watchful of his schemes. Watchful—but not fearful—we need to resist the cunning wiles of the enemy and stand firm in our faith.

Once we have a personal relationship with Jesus Christ, we are always saved. Period. End of story. The devil cannot do anything to change that except try to make us miserable, play mind games with us, and make us doubt ourselves. He seeks to render us ineffective as Christians so that we take our focus off of God and doubt His goodness and trustworthiness.

Jesus Has Overcome the Enemy

In contrast, we see that Jesus came that we would have a full and abundant life. Even though we have an enemy, there is good news: Jesus Christ came to conquer our enemy and to set the captives free so that we may experience a rich, full, abundant life.

Read Isaiah 61:1-3:

> The Spirit of the Lord God is upon me, because the Lord has anointed me to bring good news to the poor; he has sent me to bind up the brokenhearted, to proclaim liberty to the captives, and the opening of the prison to those who are bound; to proclaim the year of the Lord's favor, and the day of vengeance of our God; to comfort all who mourn; to grant to those who mourn in Zion—to give them a beautiful headdress instead of ashes, the oil of gladness instead of mourning, the garment of praise instead of a faint spirit; that they may be called oaks of righteousness, the planting of the Lord, that he may be glorified.

Review the Isaiah 61 passage and fill in the blanks.

_____ those who mourn.
To give them _____ for ashes.
The oil of _____ instead of mourning.
The garment of _____ instead of a faint spirit.

The enemy is bent on our destruction, but Jesus had different plans for his children. He sacrificed himself to save us so that we can walk in the freedom and fullness that He provides. I don't know about you, but I sure want to walk in the freedom and fullness of Christ.

Jesus sees every tear we cry and is near to those with broken hearts. He came to free us from the yoke of bondage and to set captives free, all those whom the enemy has tried to ensnare. Through Him, we get beauty from ashes as Jesus turns our tears into joy. With Jesus, nothing is ever wasted. He can transform every disappointment in our life and use it for good. Jesus is not only our rescuer, He is the lover of our souls.

Be Prepared

Let's see what else we can learn about our enemy and how we should respond. Consider 1 Peter 5:8-10.

What are we told to do in 1 Peter 5:8?

_____

_____

What does 1 Peter 5:9-10 tell us to do?

_____

_____

We are to be on guard against our enemy the devil, who is bent on our destruction. 1 Peter tells us to resist him and stand firm in our faith. As Christians, we do not have to fear him. Instead, we need to be aware of his schemes and stand firm against him.

Satan Even Tried to Tempt Jesus

Read Matthew 4:1-11.

What does Satan say to try to tempt Jesus in Matthew 4:3?

_____

How does Jesus respond?

_____

Again, Satan tempts Jesus in verses 6 and 9. What does Satan say to try to tempt Jesus in Matthew 4:9?

_____

Satan wanted Jesus, the King of Kings, to bow down and submit to him. I love Jesus's response in verse 10: "Be gone, Satan! For it is written, You shall worship the Lord your God, and him only shall you serve.'"

What an incredible example. Jesus shows us how to stand against Satan by telling him to flee and quotes scripture to back it up. We can use scripture, like Jesus did, to defend ourselves from the devil's attacks and remind him that he is a defeated foe.

Satan will whisper lies to us in order to get us to doubt God, doubt ourselves, or discourage us and render us ineffective. Fortunately, we have divine power through Christ to defeat him!

Declarations

Lord, Your Spirit is within me. You have anointed me to share the gospel message and the good news of what you have done in my life.

Jesus, you came to set captives free and to comfort all who mourn.

You exchange the mess of my life for a message of hope.

You give me beauty for ashes and replace my mourning with gladness.

You call me righteous so that *You* may be glorified.

Exchange my faint spirit for a heart full of Your praise.

Lord, help me to be aware of the schemes of the enemy. Help me to resist temptation and be filled with faith.

Overcoming in Your Life

What is holding you back from living the abundant life that Jesus came to offer? Is there anything that you need to let go of in order to pursue an abundant life?

_____

_____

Take some time to ponder and identify some of the lies the enemy has used to try to defeat you. (Examples: patterns of wrong thinking, poor attitudes.)

_____

_____

Now, replace those lies with words of truth you can use to combat the lies of the enemy.

_____

_____

We defeat our enemy when we learn to replace his lies with the truth of the word of God.

We will learn all about this in tomorrow's lesson.
Thank you, Jesus!

you are a warrior

DAY 5

Victorious warriors win first and then go to war, while defeated warriors go to war first and then seek to win. –Sun Tzu[16]

How can we fight this battle against Satan? What is our defense?

Imagine with me, for a moment, that you are a warrior preparing for battle. When soldiers prepare for war, do they go into battle unequipped or ill-prepared? No! I have watched enough History Channel television and movies to know the answer. From medieval armor to missiles and tanks, a soldier always readies for the fight with the weapons they have available. They gear up with a helmet, protective body armor, combat boots, and weapons.

Weapons are one of the most critical parts of a soldier's gear. It is essential that a warrior is fully equipped to engage in battle. Each piece of armor is crucial to combat their enemy. The victorious Christian soldier has an arsenal of weapons at his or her disposal to use in the fight against the enemy.

What My Husband's Love of the Military Has Taught Me

My husband loves watching television shows about the military. He knows everything there is to know about their equipment. Whenever I sit down and watch a show with him, he always comments on their gear. He will say, "That guy is carrying a such-and-such, and you know who makes those vests is this company," or "that is this kind of knife or gun." He even critiques how they perform their tasks on the mission, judging whether they are accurate representations or merely acting.

His love for all things military has led him to research their gear. He knows what every type of weapon does and who makes it. Most of the time, I have no idea what he is talking about, but what I have observed—and what has fascinated me—is that he knows all of the ins-and-outs of the military weapons. We, too, should be so acquainted with the tools and weapons we have at our disposal as Christian soldiers that we know exactly what each piece of equipment is and how best to use it.

Armor of God

We learn about the weapons available to us in Ephesians 6:10-20, which talks about Christians putting on the whole armor of God.

In the passage below, underline each part of the armor and its use.

> Finally, be strong in the Lord and in the strength of his might. Put on the whole armor of God, that you may be able to stand against the schemes of the devil. For we do not wrestle against flesh and blood, but against the rulers, against the authorities, against the cosmic powers over this present darkness, against the spiritual forces of evil in the heavenly places. Therefore take up the whole armor of God, that you may be able to withstand in the evil day, and having done all, to stand firm. Stand therefore, having fastened on the belt of truth, and having put on the breastplate of righteousness, and, as shoes for your feet, having put on the readiness given by the gospel of peace. In all circumstances take up the shield of faith, with which you can extinguish all the flaming darts of the evil one; and take the helmet of salvation, and the sword of the Spirit, which is the Word of God, praying at all times in the Spirit, with all prayer and supplication. To that end keep alert with all perseverance, making supplication for all the saints, and also for me, that words may be given to me in opening my mouth boldly to proclaim the mystery of the gospel, for which I am an ambassador in chains, that I may declare it boldly, as I ought to speak.

In this passage, Paul describes our battle. Who is the enemy that we are battling against?

_____

_____

How do we defeat our enemy? What weapons do we have in our arsenal?

_____

_____

Our strength comes from the power and might of the Lord because, in our own strength, we cannot withstand the schemes of the enemy. We need to put the armor of God on each day. This passage teaches and reminds us to be strong in the Lord and the strength of His might. We do not have to rely on our own ability to fight this battle; we have the backing of our all-powerful Lord to stand against the schemes of the devil. The only way for us to win this battle is to fight with the heavenly weapons God has provided!

The Belt of Truth

The first piece of armor that we are told to put on is the belt of truth. Let's take a look at some scriptures about truth.

What do we learn about truth in John 8:32?

_____

_____

What does Psalm 119:160 say about truth?

_____

_____

In John 17:17, what do we learn about God's word?

_____

_____

Breastplate of Righteousness

Once we have put on our belt of truth, we are then reminded to put on the breastplate of righteousness. The breastplate covers our vital organs and our heart.

Let's look at a few verses about righteousness and see what else we can learn.

What do we learn about armor in Isaiah 59:17?

_____

_____

What are the character qualities seen in the belt in Isaiah 11:5?

_____

_____

Now that we have our belt of truth and our breastplate of righteousness in place, we are ready to add the next piece of our armor.

Shoes of Peace

What good would any soldier be without the proper footwear? And what girl doesn't like a good pair of shoes? In this battle, we have shoes of peace for our feet.

When does 2 Timothy 4:2 say we should be prepared to share the gospel?

_____

_____

Take a look at 1 Peter 3:15. Notice when we should share the gospel:

"But in your hearts honor Christ the Lord as holy, _always being prepared_ to make a defense to anyone who asks you for a reason for the hope that is in you; yet do it with gentleness and respect" (emphasis mine).

Shield of Faith

Now that we have donned the belt of truth, our Christian body armor, and proper footwear, let's take a look at what else Paul tells us we need. He says that in _all_ circumstances we are to take up the shield of faith. It is the shield of faith that protects us from the flaming darts of the evil one.

I love the illustration given in the study notes of the ESV Study Bible, "Burning arrows were designed to destroy wooden shields and other defenses, but the shield of faith is able to extinguish the devil's attacks."[17]

Our faith is one of the most important weapons that we can utilize against the schemes of the enemy. We will look at faith more in-depth as we progress further into the study.

The Helmet of Salvation

Let's look at the final two pieces of armor: the helmet of salvation and the sword of the Spirit. We obtain the helmet of salvation when we become a Christian and confess that Jesus Christ is our Lord and Savior. Are you confident of your salvation? Do you know where you will spend eternity? If you do not know Jesus as your personal Lord and Savior, stop and pray right now, asking Him to be the Lord of your life.

There are no magic words you need to say. Just speak from your heart a simple prayer, acknowledging that Jesus Christ came to earth and died upon a cross for your sins, that He has been raised from the dead and ascended into heaven, where He is now seated at the right hand of God. Believe that Jesus died to save you from your sins and that you put your faith and trust in him alone. Once you have taken this step, you now wear the helmet of salvation and know where you will spend eternity.

Angels in heaven are rejoicing!

The Sword of the Spirit

As Christians, the weapon we wield is the sword of the Spirit—the word of God—and it is our only defensive weapon.

Look up Hebrews 4:12 and record what it says about the word of God.

_____

_____

The word of God is alive and active; Hebrews says that it is sharper than any two-edged sword. If we are to wield this powerful weapon we have been given, then we must know what the word says. We do this by reading the word, meditating on the word, and memorizing the word. When we hide God's word in our heart, we are ready to answer the hope that is within us.

In Matthew Henry's commentary, he writes, "The work of the ministry is a spiritual warfare with spiritual enemies, and for spiritual purposes. We need to be on guard against the schemes of the enemy and walk in the Spirit and pray in Spirit so that we can effect outcomes in the physical realm."[18]

If we want to live a victorious life and be an overcomer, we must put on the whole armor of God.

Are you suited up for battle today friend?

Declarations

I am a warrior. I am strong in the Lord because He is strong and He lives within me. When I am weak, Jesus makes me strong.

I will suit up every day and put on my armor to fight against the schemes of the enemy.

God, Your word is true, it is a powerful weapon, and it sets me free.

Help me to meditate on and memorize Your word in order to fight against the enemy's fiery arrows.

Overcoming in Your Life

Let's review the six pieces of armor we are told to put on daily. Jot them down below.

_____
_____
_____
_____
_____
_____

When you have bad days or experience tough seasons, what do you do to keep your eyes focused on Jesus?

_____

_____

How do you put on the armor of God? What does that look like in your daily life?

_____

_____

Do you see yourself as a warrior?

_____

_____

Press on and fight the good fight. You are a warrior with mighty weapons at your disposal. We are victorious over every scheme of the enemy. Through Jesus Christ and the power of his shed blood, we can overcome anything that comes against us. We have learned so much this week about the battle we are in and what it means to overcome. I am so proud of your progress!

Let's close with the comforting words of Psalm 91:

> He who dwells in the shelter of the Most High will abide in the shadow of the Almighty. I will say to the Lord, "My refuge and my fortress, my God, in whom I trust."
>
> For he will deliver you from the snare of the fowler and from the deadly pestilence. He will cover you with his pinions, and under his wings you will find refuge; his faithfulness is a shield and buckler.
>
> You will not fear the terror of the night; nor the arrow that flies by day, nor the pestilence that stalks in darkness, nor the destruction that wastes at noonday.
>
> A thousand may fall at your side, ten thousand at your right hand, but it will not come near you. You will only look with your eyes and see the recompense of the wicked.
>
> Because you have made the Lord your dwelling place—the Most High, who is my refuge—no evil shall be allowed to befall you, no plague come near your tent.
>
> For he will command his angels concerning you to guard you in all your ways. On their hands they will bear you up, lest you strike your foot against a stone. You will tread on the lion and the adder; the young lion and the serpent you will trample underfoot.
>
> "Because he holds fast to me in love, I will deliver him; I will protect him, because he knows my name.
>
> When he calls to me, I will answer him; I will be with him in trouble; I will rescue him and honor him.
>
> With long life I will satisfy him and show him my salvation."

I hope those verses give you as much comfort as they give me, knowing that God is my refuge and fortress. He will deliver me from the schemes of the enemy because He is faithful, and He will deliver you too my friend.

Week 2

OUR PROBLEM

weapons of warfare

DAY 1

The Christian life is a battle. Day by day you are engaged in warfare. You must remember this each morning when you crawl from beneath the sheets. Whether you do or not will have a lot to do with how the battle goes that day! [1]

Powerful God Tools

My husband has a garage full of tools, hammers, screwdrivers, pliers, and all manner of power tools for any job you can imagine. Each tool is built for a specific task. If he sends me to the garage to get a Torx head screwdriver to take the freezer handle off, and I bring back a Phillips or flat head driver to him, he'll get annoyed with me for bringing the wrong tool and will be unable to use it for his task. The tool has to fit the need to be useful.

Likewise, I have a kitchen full of utensils. If I am cooking and need to stir a pot, but never get a spoon out of the drawer, I will ruin what I am cooking. God's word is like both of these examples: we have to use the tools we have been given in scripture to combat the lies of our enemy. We also have to know the right tool to use, which is why it is important to know what the word of God says.

Walk Like a Soldier

Our Christian walk is a battlefield, and we are front-line soldiers in the war for our lives. We need to know as much as we can about our enemy and understand the resources we have available for us to use in our fight.

Yesterday, we spent time learning about the armor of God and the weapons we have in our arsenal. As we conclude this week's study, we are going to focus on one central passage of scripture but look at it through the lens of three different versions of the Bible.

As believers, we may still carry habits and mindsets of our old life. Because of this, we must habitually shed our old nature and put on our new nature. Today, let's look at 2 Corinthians 10:3-5 and see what else we can learn about our enemy and our weapons of warfare.

What does 2 Corinthians 10:3-5 tell us about our warfare?

_____

_____

In this passage of scripture, the apostle Paul defends his ministry. Paul says that we are not battling flesh and blood, we are fighting a spiritual battle. He says that our weapons of warfare have divine power to tear down and destroy strongholds.

These verses in Corinthians remind us that we have divine power to destroy strongholds, arguments, and any lofty opinion that goes against the knowledge of God.

Do not miss what it says at the end of the second verse—*we are to take each thought captive to the obedience of Christ*. This means we should compare every thought that enters our mind to the truth of scripture. Through the divine power we have been given, we can change our wrong thinking that leads to wrong behavior and, instead, conform ourselves to Christ.

Our earthly bodies are made of flesh. Therefore, we walk in the flesh, but our warfare is spiritual. The armor of God helps us stand against the evil one. Through prayer, the word of God, faith, and the power of the Holy Spirit, we have divine power to take our thoughts captive to the obedience of Christ and to tear down strongholds of wrong thinking and behavior. We must also get rid of anything in our lives that tries to take the place of God or becomes an idol to us.

If we are to live a victorious Christian life, we need to replace the lies the enemy tells us about ourselves with the truth. We need to believe the truth of who the Lord says we are and rise like warriors against the schemes of the enemy. We need to know that Jesus is our Savior and Lord, and understand that he offers love, peace, forgiveness, righteousness, deliverance, an example to us, companionship, guardianship, security, sufficiency, fulfillment, and so much more. Jesus is everything!

Finally, read 2 Corinthians 10:3-6 in The Message Bible:

> The world is unprincipled. It's dog-eat-dog out there! The world doesn't fight fair. But we don't live or fight our battles that way—we never have and never will. The tools of our trade aren't for marketing or manipulation, but they are for demolishing that entire massively corrupt culture. We use our powerful God-tools for smashing warped philosophies, tearing down barriers erected against the truth of God, and fitting every loose thought and emotion and impulse into the structure of life shaped by Christ. Our tools are ready for clearing the ground of every obstruction and building lives of obedience into maturity.

I love the emphasis this version adds to this passage. We learn from a very early age that life isn't always fair, but aren't you glad you have powerful God-given tools that are able to smash warped philosophies and help us stand against our massively corrupt culture? His truths are able to tear down barriers erected against his promises, so that we may live a life shaped by Christ.

When we experience difficulties, we can be tempted to question God's plan for our lives or wallow in our circumstances. We ask, "Why me?" Some people even question the very goodness of God. In these times, we must focus on Jesus instead of our situation.

Counting Your Gifts

I began reading *One Thousand Gifts: A Dare to Live Fully Right Where You Are* by Ann Voskamp right around the time I found out I was pregnant with my son Liam. I found out I was pregnant a few weeks before my fortieth birthday. Because of my complicated history and my age, I was considered a high-risk pregnancy and was closely monitored from the beginning. We opted out of having an amniocentesis or any other genetic testing. At a routine ultrasound, we found out that our son had a heart defect and likely had some kind of chromosomal abnormality. Our worst fears were confirmed, and several weeks later, our son was stillborn.

Because I was reading *One Thousand Gifts*, I was in the habit of practicing daily gratitude. I thanked God for every day I was pregnant. Every time I felt nausea; every time I felt the baby kick.
Practicing daily gratitude, despite facing one of the most difficult circumstances a mom could ever face, changed everything. I was able to maintain a heavenly perspective in light of my

difficult earthly circumstances. My friends would call me on the phone to check on me, and instead of ministering to me, I would comfort them because I was filled with the peace that passes understanding.

Friend, I don't know what you are going through today, but what I do know is that the spiritual discipline of practicing gratitude and cultivating a life of praise and thanksgiving changes everything.

The Importance of Praise and Thanksgiving

Recently, I was preparing to speak in front of a large audience, and I was quite nervous. In fact, I was so nervous that I was to the point of making myself physically ill. As I sat with a friend, asking for prayer, I told her how I was meditating on Philippians 4:6-7. It reads: "Do not be anxious about anything, but in everything by prayer and supplication with thanksgiving let your requests be made known to God. And the peace of God, which surpasses all understanding, will guard your hearts and your minds in Christ Jesus."

I told her that even though I'd been meditating on this verse, I couldn't shake the anxiety. She said, "Misty, you are praying and mediating on scripture, but don't forget the thanksgiving! You need to begin praising God." In that moment, everything changed. I began praising God for the opportunity to speak to speak at my church. I thanked him for all of the women that I would be speaking to from the stage. I praised him for everything I could think of, and suddenly my anxiety began to fade.

One of the best ways to take my eyes off my situation and gain a proper perspective is to praise God. Remember, we were created to worship Him! I don't know about you, but I love music of all kinds. Praise and worship songs, contemporary Christian music, and hymns all minister to my soul.

Praising God helps me to regain a proper perspective on God and the faithfulness he provides.

Declarations

The battle I am in today is a spiritual battle.

I need to be careful about where I allow my mind to go.

I must police my thoughts by taking them captive to the obedience of Christ.

Through the power of Christ, I have an arsenal of powerful weapons to demolish strongholds in my life.

Every stronghold will be broken in the name of Jesus.

I will praise God in the midst of my battle. I will not be anxious. Instead, I will choose to believe the word of God and His truth for my life.

Overcoming in Your Life

Thank God that we can live a victorious life through His word and by His divine power! We have mighty weapons at our disposal that can help us stand against our enemy. Praise the Lord; He is worthy of our praise!

What helps you keep your eyes on Jesus during difficult times?

_____

_____

How can the word of God help you live a victorious life in your everyday circumstances?

_____

_____

the problem

DAY 2

Lord keep us all from sin. Teach us how to walk circumspectly; enable us to guard our minds against error of doctrine, our hearts against wrong feelings, and our lives against evil actions. –Charles Spurgeon[2]

Let's take a minute to review what we have learned so far.

Who is our battle against? What must we overcome?

_____

_____

In today's lesson, we are going to take a closer look at the problem of sin. From the beginning, that problem has plagued us, and we must do everything we can overcome it.

According to *Systematic Theology* by Wayne Grudeum, "Sin is a failure to conform to the moral law of God in act, attitude or nature."[3] Sin is not only doing what is wrong–for example, stealing–but also the heart attitude that motivates the action. God sees beyond our actions and straight to our heart. He knows our motives.

Original Sin

In previous lessons, we learned that our battle is against the devil, who deceived Adam and Eve in the Garden. It was at that point that sin entered the world and caused Adam and Eve to question God's goodness.

This lapse is frequently called the "original" sin. Before we delve any further into the scriptures, I think it is important to establish the fact that God did not sin himself. Instead, rebellion against God brought sin into the world.

Systematic Theology explains this further, "First, we must clearly affirm that God himself did not sin, and God is not to be blamed for sin. It was man who sinned, and it was angels who sinned, and in both cases, they did so by willful, voluntary choice. To blame for God for sin would be blasphemy against the character of God."[4] We cannot blame God for our wrongdoing. Our sin is a willful act of disobedience against God.

In Romans 5:12, what do we learn about sin and death?

_____

_____

Sin entered the world through Adam and Eve and brought with it the consequence of death, which spread to all men, because we are all sinners.

What is Sin?

When we believe anything that is contrary to the word of God, we sin.

According to the ESV Study Bible, "Sin is anything (whether in thoughts, actions or attitudes) that does not express or conform to the holy character of God as expressed in his moral law."[5]

Sin is anything that goes against God's Law.

What do we learn about sin in Romans 14:23?

_____

_____

Faith is belief in God, and anything that is not of God is sin. Our God is holy, righteous, and just. As humans, our sin separates us from Him. These ideas are exemplified in the following verses:

Our sin separates us from him. Isaiah 59:2 says, "But your inquiries have made a separation between you and your God, and your sins have hidden his face from you so that He does not hear."

The Lord is righteous and holy. Psalm 145:17 declares, "The LORD is righteous in all his ways and kind in all his works." Isaiah 6:1 exclaims, "Holy, holy, holy is the Lord of hosts; the whole earth is full of his glory." Because He is holy and righteous, He cannot even look upon our sin. Habakkuk 1:13 says, "You who are of purer than to see evil and can not look at wrong."

Biblical Terms for Sin

There are several biblical terms for sin. According to the ESV Study Bible, "The Bible explains human rebellion against God from several perspectives and with various images."[6] Look up the following verses in the ESV translation. (If you don't have a copy of the ESV, then you can look it up online.) Note what sin is called in each scripture.

In Judges 2:11, what image is used to describe sin?

_____

What term is used to describe sin in Romans 5:19?

_____

What word is used to describe sin in Exodus 23:21 and 1 Timothy 2:14?

_____

What does Leviticus 26:40 call sin?

_____

In both Titus 2:14 and 1 John 3:4, what word is used to describe sin?

_____

The word used in Ephesians 2:1 for sin is:

_____

How does 1 Peter 4:18 refer to sin?

_____

How is sin described in 1 John 1:9?

_____

In 1 Timothy 1:9, we see the word _____ to illustrate sin.

Proverbs 11:31 calls sin _____.

Sin in these verses is characterized as evil, disobedience, transgression, iniquity, lawlessness, trespasses, ungodliness, unrighteousness, unholy, and wickedness. No matter what we call it, sin is our problem. It is the thing we all must struggle to overcome.

Thankfully, God did not leave us on our own to deal with our problem. He provided a solution in the form of his son Jesus. When we put our faith and trust in Jesus, we confess our sin and repent. When we turn away from our sins, we are able to walk in the newness of life in Christ.

Declarations

I humble myself before a holy and righteous God and turn away from sin.

I believe God is able to cleanse me from all unrighteousness.

My faith and trust are in Jesus Christ alone.

Overcoming in Your Life

Sin is anything that causes us to distrust God or question His goodness, mercy, grace, and love. We need to keep a short account of our sins with God. Through Jesus, our sins can be forgiven, but it is our job to confess our sins.

Considering all that you have learned today about sin, is there anything between you and God that you need to confess and repent of today?

_____
_____
_____
_____

 Prayer

Heavenly Father, you are a good, good Father. Thank you so much that you did not leave us to our own devices in the struggle against sin. Instead, you understand our frail human condition and have mercy on us. We thank you for your son, Jesus Christ. We are humbled that he was beaten, bruised, and suffered a humiliating death on a cross to pay the penalty for our sin. Lord, convict us of our sin. Help us in our weakness so we may quickly repent. Create in us a clean heart, Lord. We praise you, in Jesus's name!

tactics of the enemy

DAY 3

Know thy self, know thy enemy. A thousand battles, a thousand victories.
–Sun Tzu, *The Art of War*[7]

As we discussed earlier, we are participants in the battle of the ages that began in the Garden of Eden. We must always be aware that we are in a war against a very real enemy.

I love the way my friend Sheryl from *Simply Scripture* phrased this principle in her Bible study on the book of Jude:

> We have an insidious spiritual enemy that is lurking and we are being caught off guard simply because it is dressed nicely as socially acceptable and politically correct. Dear sister, you are not on a playground, and this is not a game. You are on a battlefield where the enemy has a bullseye on real people and plays for keep. Girl, get in your Bible and know what it says! Pick it up and learn it![8]

Let's look at what we learn about our enemy by filling in the blanks for the following verses.

In John 10:10, "The _____ comes only to _____ and _____ and _____." In contrast, the verse ends with this declaration, "I [Jesus] came that they may have _____ and have it abundantly."

The devil is described as a thief who is bent on our destruction. He wants to steal our joy—our love for one another—by destroying our families, our relationships, and anything else that brings glory to the Lord. Yet we know that nothing can steal our salvation. The devil can't do anything to change our relationship with the Lord, but he *can* try to make us miserable and ineffective Christians. He attempts to take our focus and trust off of God. In contrast to the devil's life-stealing schemes, Jesus came that we would have a full and abundant life.

Lord, I want to live the abundant life you came to give me.

Let's see what else we can learn about our enemy and how we should respond.

1 Peter 5:8 says, "Be sober minded; be watchful. Your _____ the _____ prowls around like a roaring lion, seeking someone to devour."

We are to be on guard against our adversary, who is bent on our destruction. However, as Christians, we do not have to be afraid of him.

1 Peter 5:9-10 goes on to say, "Resist him, firm in your faith, knowing that the same kinds of suffering are being experienced by your brotherhood throughout the world. And after you have suffered a little while, the God of all grace, who has called you to his eternal glory in Christ, will himself restore, confirm, strengthen, and establish you."

Scripture reminds us to stand firm against the enemy's schemes, remaining vigilant in our battle against him. As Matthew Henry's *Commentary* notes,

> The whole design of Satan is to devour and destroy our souls. He always is contriving whom he may ensnare to eternal ruin. Our duty plainly is, to be sober; to govern both the outward and the inward man by the rules of temperance. To be vigilant; suspicious of constant danger from this spiritual enemy, watchful and diligent to prevent his designs.[9]

We must be watchful but not fearful. We need to resist the cunning wiles of the enemy and stand firm in our faith. Have you ever heard the expression, "knowledge is power"? Let's dig into the scriptures and see what else can we learn from the Bible about sin so we can be armed with the truth.

More on Sin

Begin by reading more about sin in the following verses.

What does James 4:7 say about doing the right thing and sin?

_____

In 1 John 1:8-10, what must we do so that our sins are forgiven?

_____

According to Romans 3:23, who has sinned?

_____

Contrast the wages of sin and the gift from God in Romans 6:23.

_____

What does 1 John 5:17 call sin? _____

James 1:15 says that desire leads to sin, and sin leads to _____.

Read Psalm 51:1-5:

> Have mercy on me, O God, according to your steadfast love;
> according to your abundant mercy blot out my transgressions.
> Wash me thoroughly from my iniquity, and cleanse me from my sin!
> For I know my transgressions, and my sin is ever before me.
> Against you, you only, have I sinned and done what is evil in your sight,
> so that you may be justified in your words and blameless in your judgment.
> Behold, I was brought forth in iniquity, and in sin did my mother conceive me.

Who does David say he has sinned against?

_____

At what point are we considered sinful, according to Psalm 51:5?

_____

What else do we learn from this passage?

_____

Submit Yourself to God

We can resist the temptation to sin when we submit ourselves to God. We have all sinned and fallen short of the glory of God, and deceive ourselves if we think that we do not sin. However, there is good news—if we confess our sin to God, He is faithful to forgive us and cleanse us from our unrighteousness. God doesn't give us what we deserve. The penalty for sin is death, but the gracious gift of God is eternal life through Jesus Christ, our Lord and Savior. Praise Him!

I don't know about you, but more often than not, it is not outright, willful sin that trips me up. I don't steal or murder, but I have wicked thoughts, experience wrong thinking, or indulge in attitudes that cause me to sin. Sometimes, my attitude just plain stinks. I fuss at my kids or get upset with my husband, and I have to repent of my sinful behavior and ask for their forgiveness more times than I care to admit.

What does Romans 12:2 say we should do?

_____

_____

_____

The New Living Translation tells us, "Don't copy the behavior and customs of this world, but let God transform you into a new person by changing the way you think. Then you will learn to know God's will for you, which is good, and pleasing, and perfect."

When we read and meditate on scripture, it changes us and makes more like Christ.

If you are struggling with sin in your life, confess it to God. When you humble yourself before Him, He is faithful to forgive you and will transform your life.

Declarations

God, I submit my will to You.

I will be mindful and watchful—but not fearful—of the enemy's schemes.

Devil, in the name of Jesus, I resist you! You must flee.

I confess my sins because I know God is faithful and just to forgive my sins and cleanse me from all unrighteousness.

Overcoming in Your Life

What is holding you back from living the abundant life that Jesus came to give? Are there things or people in your life with whom you struggle or that seek to take first place in your life? If so, confess your struggle to prioritize to Jesus now.

_____
_____
_____
_____

Conclude today's lesson by writing out a prayer of repentance.

_____
_____
_____

Praise Jesus for saving us from the penalty of our sins. Although we deserved death for our sins, we have instead been offered eternal life, and now rest secure in the knowledge that He forgives and cleanses us from our sin!

DAY 4

Sin and forgiveness and falling and getting back up and losing the pearl of great price in the couch cushions but then finding it again, and again, and again? Those are the stumbling steps to becoming Real, the only script that's really worth following in this world or the one that's coming. —Brennan Manning[10]

We live in a fallen world and experience the effects of evil and sin in a lot of different ways. Scripture teaches us that those occurrences will continue to escalate in the last days, as the love of many people toward the things of God will grow cold. Instead of a healthy respect for God and his truth, we will see sin manifest itself in the world in myriad ways. If you have any doubts about whether or not this process has already begun, just turn on the nightly news or read the daily headlines.

The Last Days

According to Acts 2:17, when did the last days begin?

_____

_____

The last days began when God poured out his spirit to mankind at Pentecost and continue through our present day. That means we are living in the last days. We need to understand the times in which we live.

Read the passage below and note how sin is manifested in the last days.

> But realize this, that in the last days difficult times will come. For men will be lovers of self, lovers of money, boastful, arrogant, revilers, disobedient to parents, ungrateful, unholy, unloving, irreconcilable, malicious gossips, without self-control, brutal, haters of good, treacherous, reckless, conceited, lovers of pleasure rather than lovers of God, holding to a form of godliness, although they have denied its power; Avoid such men as these. (2 Timothy 3:1-6)

Notice the first thing this verse says: **In the last days, difficult times will come.**

We are to recognize and watch out for the ugly behaviors that are listed because scripture warns us that they will happen. The verse lists several negative attributes of man, and as believers, we are told to avoid people who exhibit these characteristics:

Lovers of self
Lovers of money
Boastful
Arrogant
Revilers
Disobedient to parents
Ungrateful
Unholy
Unloving
Irreconcilable
Malicious gossips
Without self-control
Brutal
Haters of good
Treacherous
Reckless
Conceited
Lovers of pleasure rather than lovers of God

Let us not despair when we see evil in our world today

Look at the list above and circle any characteristics that you see in the world today.

According to *Benson's Commentary*, "The vices mentioned in this and the two following verses have always existed in the world. But they're being spoken of here as characteristic of the latter days, implies that, besides being common in these days, they would be openly avowed and defended."[11]

Can you think of some areas of sin that are openly avowed and justified today?

_____
_____
_____
_____

When we consider the world around us, we see more and more people exhibit these attributes. We find a similar list in Romans 1:29-31: "They were filled with all manner of unrighteousness, evil, covetousness, malice. They are full of envy, murder, strife, deceit, maliciousness. They are gossips, slanderers, haters of God, insolent, haughty, boastful, inventors of evil, disobedient to parents, foolish, faithless, heartless, ruthless."

Circle any of these sins you see present in our world today.

Unrighteousness	Evil	Covetousness
Malice	Envy	Murder
Strife	Deceit	Maliciousness
Gossips	Slanderers	Haters of God
Insolent	Haughty	Boastful
Inventors of evil	Disobedient to Parents	Foolish
Faithless	Heartless	Ruthless

What is the cause of problems today? Frankly, we have a sin problem. All of the problems that we recognize are a result of humanity turning against God and his law in rebellion.

Aren't you so glad this is not the end of the story? Let us not despair when we see evil in our world today. Jesus came to our rescue in the midst of our sin, and God is faithful to us and loves us more than we know. He is redeeming us and all things to himself.

More Characteristics of the Last Days

What does the Spirit say in 1 Timothy 4:1?

_____
_____
_____
_____

What do we learn from 1 Timothy 4:3?

_____
_____

Who will the scoffers follow, according to Jude 1:18?

_____
_____

What do we learn from 2 Peter 3:3?

_____
_____

We should not be surprised when we see troubling events happening in our world today. The Bible has warned us that in the last days, men will be lovers of self, forego sound doctrine, and instead will seek teaching that tickles their ears.

When we see evil things happening, what should our response be?

_____
_____

I believe we can look to Hebrews 10:23-25 for our answer:

"Let us hold fast the confession of our hope without wavering, for he who promised is faithful. And let us consider how to stir up one another to love and good works, not neglecting to meet together, as is the habit of some, but encouraging one another, and all the more as you see the Day drawing near."

Matthew Henry's _Commentary_ says, "The purified minds of Christians are to be stirred up, that they may be active and lively in the work of holiness. There will be scoffers in the last days, under the gospel, men who make light of sin, and mock at salvation by Jesus Christ."[12]

We have to hold on to hope and remember the great promises we have available to us in Jesus.

He is faithful. We must surround ourselves with Christian brothers and sisters who will hold us accountable and speak the truth to us in love—people who will encourage us, pray for and with us, and remind us of the truth of God's word.

Jesus will return soon, but until that day arrives, we need to encourage one another in our Christian walk of faith. We should busy ourselves with our Father's business of loving others, caring for widows and orphans, visiting the sick and imprisoned, sharing the good news of Jesus Christ, gathering with other believers, and doing good works.

Declarations

I understand the time in which I live. I choose today to stand strong in my faith and turn away from sin.

Lord, You are holy, righteous, and true. Show me where I fall short.

I humble myself before You, Lord. I confess I am a sinner. Save me from sin and all unrighteousness.

Overcoming in Your Life

Let's conclude our lesson by spending some time examining our hearts and minds for any thoughts, attitudes, or actions that resemble the negative behavior of those described in the last days.

Because we live in a fallen world, we are surrounded by the corrupting nature of sin. The behaviors we identified today should cause us to look inward and reflect on our heart condition. Self-examination is a necessary practice in the victorious Christian walk.

Ask God to reveal the root problem of sin in your life so that you can confess your sin and He can forgive you.

_____

_____

_____

_____

Remember that God loves us in spite of our sin. Sin separates us from God and his holiness, yet He came to save us while we were sinners. He loves us and wants to be in relationship with us. May we always be thankful that He has promised to be faithful!

I am so grateful to be on this Bible study journey with you. Know that I am praying for you and am cheering you on.

Press on, dear sister. Press on.

DAY 5

God teaches you the way of love by loving you well. He loves you with patience and kindness. He loves you by never giving up or walking out on you. God loves you perfectly because He is love. —Jennifer Rothschild[13]

Over the past week, we examined the human predicament—the problem of sin. The original rebellion against God started in heaven when the angels rebelled against God. It then manifested itself in the Garden of Eden when Adam and Eve rebelled against God at Satan's urging. Yet rebellion still plagues us today and is most easily identified in the way our sin separates us from a holy and just God. It is only through Christ's atoning sacrifice on the cross that we are reconciled to God and can be in a right relationship with Him.

There is good news! Let's begin today by contrasting the sin we discussed in our previous lesson (more specifically, the characteristics of men seen in the last days) to the attributes of God. Where we will begin to explore the answers to our sin problem.

Attributes of God

In 1 John 4, we learn that God is love. Underline every instance of the word "love" in the following passage:

> Beloved, let us love one another, for love is from God, and whoever loves has been born of God and knows God. Anyone who does not love does not know God because God is love. In this the love of God was made manifest among us, that God sent his only Son into the world, so that we might live through him. In this is love, not that we have loved God but that he loved us and sent his Son to be the propitiation for our sins. Beloved, if God so loved us, we also ought to love one another. No one has ever seen God; if we love one another, God abides in us and his love is perfected in us. (1 John 4:7-12)

What does this passage tell us to do? Why?

_____

_____

Who loves God?

_____

_____

What do we learn about those who don't love God?

_____

_____

From these passages, we learn that love comes from God. Whoever loves has been born of God. Therefore, we should love one another. We will win others to Christ because of our genuine love for them and our love for Christ.

If you do not love, you do not know God. God is love. He loves us so much that He sent His one and only son to die for our sins and reconcile us to Himself. We are His prized creation and we were made for love.

The Love Passage

1 John 4:7-12 is similar to the love passage of 1 Corinthians 13. Let's look at the Corinthians passage to see what else we can learn about love.

Underline every reference to the word "love":

> If I speak in the tongues of men and of angels, but have not love, I am a noisy gong or a clanging cymbal. If I have prophetic powers, and understand all mysteries and all knowledge, and if I have all faith, so as to remove mountains, but have not love, I am nothing. If I give away all I have, and if I deliver up my body to be burned, but have not love, I gain nothing.
>
> Love is patient and kind; love does not envy or boast; it is not arrogant or rude. It does not insist on its own way; it is not irritable or resentful; it does not rejoice at wrongdoing, but rejoices with the truth. Love bears all things, believes all things, hopes all things, endures all things.
>
> Love never ends. As for prophecies, they will pass away; as for tongues, they will cease; as for knowledge, it will pass away. For we know in part and we prophesy in part, but when the perfect comes, the partial will pass away.
>
> When I was a child, I spoke like a child, I thought like a child, I reasoned like a child. When I became a man, I gave up childish ways. For now we see in a mirror dimly, but then face-to-face. Now I know in part; then I shall know fully, even as I have been fully known. So now faith, hope, and love abide, these three; but the greatest of these is love.

What do we learn about love from this passage?
_____
_____

Will we win others to Christ by beating them over the head with gospel? *Absolutely not!* Instead, we are told that others will know us by our love.

Love bears all things, hope all things, endures all things. Love never ends. God is love and because of His great love for us, we know what love means and are able to love others.

Fill in the blanks for 2 Peter 1:5-7:
For this very reason, make every effort to supplement your faith with _____
and virtue with _____,
and knowledge with _____-_____,
and self-control with _____,
and steadfastness with _____,
and godliness with _____
and brotherly affection with _____.

This is not a list of things we must do to get to heaven; rather, it is a beautiful expression of our faith and is evidence of a transformed heart. God has given us great promises that we may share in His divine nature. As we become more like Him, we will develop these attributes.

Read Galatians 5:16-25. In this passage, we are told to walk in the Spirit and not gratify the desires of the flesh.

Name the works of the flesh as described in verses 19-21.

_____
_____
_____
_____

Those who are in Christ will crucify their fleshly desires and start to become more Christlike. The fruits of the Spirit are contrary to our sin nature (the works of the flesh). In Galatians 5:22-23, we learn about the fruits of the Spirit.

List the fruits of the Spirit:
1._____
2._____
3._____
4._____
5._____
6._____
7._____
8._____
9._____

As Christians, these fruits are a gift to us. As we walk in the Spirit and crucify the works of the flesh, we become more conformed to the image of Jesus. The more Christlike we become, the more freedom we possess. God has called us to walk in freedom—not so that we can do whatever we want, but as a guide to assist us in loving and serving one another.

Battle Tactics

Remember, man fell prey to sin as a result of pride, arrogance, and rebellion, mirroring Satan's own fall from grace. We must recognize that we are in a real battle and that Satan is our enemy. He intends to distract us, render us ineffective, steal our joy, and use our pain and heartache in life to lead us away from God and into sin. His aim is to destroy us.

To combat the enemy, we must cling to scripture to correct the lies we are told and utilize the weapons in our arsenal.

We must put on gospel glasses so that we can properly see who we are and whose we are. We must recognize the truth that we are loved and cherished by the almighty creator of heaven and earth, and that He is on our side. By keeping our focus on God, we start to become more like Him. We overcome evil by doing good. Praise be to God!

Declarations

I am a child of God, and He loves me!

I am a Christian warrior in a battle against a real enemy.

Our enemy Satan is a defeated foe.

Greater is He who is in me than he that is in the world.

Overcoming in Your Life

What are some ways you can show love to your friends and family? Your neighbors? How about strangers or people you don't know?

_____
_____
_____
_____
_____
_____

How can you share the love of Christ with an unbeliever in your life?

_____
_____
_____

Ponder ways you can share the love of Christ in a new way this week. Jot down some ideas.

_____
_____
_____
_____

Week 3

DON'T STAND ALONE—WALK THROUGH THE OLD TESTAMENT

DAY 1

This week, we will walk through the Old Testament to look at some of the Bible's most significant overcomers. These stories serve as examples of how to live an overcoming and victorious life. We will walk through the stories of Noah, Abraham, Joseph, Moses, Job, and Daniel in order to see how each of the overcomers utilized faith in God and integrity to combat the trials they faced. Together, we will look at a sampling of the faithful heroes of the Old Testament who were victorious in their lives and discover how they exhibited victory in the midst of struggles.

We will begin by laying a foundation with a quick summary of Genesis. If you haven't read it, here's a quick overview: The Bible begins with the story of Creation. God created the heavens and the earth and everything that is in it. He created man and woman and, shortly thereafter, man sinned and fell. In the story of Cain and Abel, we learn about life under the curse of sin, as the first murder is committed.

The next story we encounter is Noah, the flood God sent to cleanse the earth, and God's covenant to never do so again.

Begin by reading Genesis 6:5 to see what we can learn about Noah and the culture of his day:

> The LORD saw that the wickedness of man was great in the earth, and that every intention of the thoughts of his heart was only evil continually. And the LORD regretted that he had made man on the earth, and it grieved him to his heart. So the LORD said, "I will blot out man whom I have created from the face of the land, man and animals and creeping things and birds of the heavens, for I am sorry that I have made them." But Noah found favor in the eyes of the LORD.

What was the cultural climate like in the time of Noah? What was the condition of man's heart?

_____
_____
_____

Does our culture today reflect the Lord's design or fallen man's desires?

_____
_____

Let's see what else we can learn about Noah. Write out the following verses:

Genesis 6:9

_____
_____

Hebrews 11:7

_____

_____

_____

Noah found favor in the eyes of God in the midst of a wicked and perverse generation, at a time when the hearts of men were continuously evil. The earth was full of violence and men were corrupt; in fact, man was so evil that the Lord regretted even creating him. So great was God's disappointment and disgust that He chose to blot out all men. He created a flood on the whole earth to destroy mankind. Only Noah found favor with the Lord, despite the wickedness and unbelief of those who surrounded him.

What does it mean that Noah "walked with God"?

_____

Did Noah physically walk with God? The Hebrew word in this passage for walked is ה ת ה (hitʰ·hal·lek) and, according to the ESV Study Bible, "The Hebrew verb for 'walked' is a distinctive form that conveys the sense of ongoing intimacy with God."

Noah knew the Lord; they had a relationship. While other men's thoughts were evil, Noah kept his heart and mind focused on God! God warned Noah about future events and, in reverent fear, Noah obeyed God. Because of his faith, Noah was seen as righteous in the eyes of God. Each day, we have a choice as to whom we will serve. We have free will and the ability to choose life or death.

The Lord told Noah to build an ark out of gopher wood and gave Noah specific instructions on how to build the ark. The Lord planned to flood the entire earth with water and wipe out every living, breathing thing that remained. The Lord instructed Noah to take his wife, his sons, and their wives into the ark along with a male and a female of every living thing. In addition, they were to take food of every kind to eat and to store.

Read Genesis 7:1. What word does God use to describe Noah in this passage?

_____

Day after day, Noah labored to build the ark. It took him 120 years to build the ark, and he spent each day warning others to repent and turn to the Lord during that time. Noah did everything the Lord instructed him to do. The Lord saved Noah and his family because Noah was righteous. In a time when everyone else was wicked, Noah lived by faith and chose to follow the Lord.

I tell my kids all the time, "I don't care if all of your friends are going left; if God tells you to go right, then you go right." They also hear me say, "You need to be who you are supposed to be and do what you know is right." One day, we will all stand before the Lord and will be accountable for our actions. On that day, we want to be found obedient and declared as righteous.

Noahic Covenant

When Noah left the ark, the Lord formed a covenant with Noah, known as the Noahic covenant. Read about the covenant in Genesis 8:1-9:17. What is the promise that was made to Noah?

_____

_____

_____

_____

After the flood, the nations were separated. Genesis 11 recounts the story of the tower of Babel. As the Old Testament narrative continues, we read a number of stories about how God calls Abram/Abraham and interacts with him in the stories of Abram and Pharaoh, Abram and Lot, the blessing of Melchizedek, and God making a covenant with Abram.

While all of these stories provide a historical foundation for our faith, the faithfulness of the characters portrayed in them provides a glimpse of the way in which God's love for us began and how it has continued to the present day. With that in mind, let's close today's lesson with some final encouraging thoughts from the Old Testament.

Joshua 24:15 says, "And if it is evil in your eyes to serve the Lord, choose this day whom you will serve, whether the gods your fathers served in the region beyond the River, or the gods of the Amorites in whose land you dwell. But as for me and my house, we will serve the Lord."

What do we learn from Deuteronomy 30:19?

_____
_____
_____

We are enticed by many things that seek to get a hold of us. Whom will we serve? We can either choose to follow Christ and live in obedience to God, which leads to blessing, or we can choose the path of lies that leads to death and destruction.

Declarations

Today, I choose to serve the Lord.

I will obey the Lord.

My obedience equals blessing.

Overcoming in Your Life

What about you, friend? Will you be found faithful? Are you willing to stand up for God in the midst of a wicked and perverse generation? Are you willing to make decisions that are countercultural to please God? Meditate on these questions as we bring this lesson to a close. Ask God how He wants you to respond to Him today.

_____
_____

Well done. Tomorrow, we will investigate the story of Abraham/Abram.

DAY 2

I believe in Christianity as I believe that the sun has risen, not only because I see it, but because by it, I see everything else. —C. S. Lewis[1]

We begin today's lesson by looking at the covenant between God and Abraham.

Read the Abrahamic covenant in Genesis 12:1-3:

> Now the Lord said to Abram, "Go from your country and your kindred and your father's house to the land that I will show you. And I will make of you a great nation, and I will bless you and make your name great, so that you will be a blessing. I will bless those who bless you, and him who dishonors you I will curse, and in you all the families of the earth shall be blessed."

Read Genesis 15:1. What did the Lord say to Abram?

_____

_____

Abram was known for his faith in God. He was told that we would be the father of many nations even though he was childless. To make matters worse, he and his wife were old—really old. Yet Abraham believed and trusted God to fulfill His promise.

In spite of his circumstances, Abraham believed the promises of God. The Abrahamic covenant promised three things:

1. Abraham and descendants would inherit the land of Canaan.
2. They would become a great nation.
3. Through them, all nations would be blessed.

The Faith of Abraham

Let's journey to the New Testament book of Hebrews and see what else we can learn about Abraham.

In Hebrews 11:8-10, we read:

> By faith Abraham obeyed when he was called to go out to a place that he was to receive as an inheritance. And he went out, not knowing where he was going. By faith he went to live in the land of promise, as in a foreign land, living in tents with Isaac and Jacob, heirs with him of the same promise. For he was looking forward to the city that has foundations, whose designer and builder is God.

Do you see the connection between Noah and Abraham? They were both men of faith who believed the word of God. They did what God told them to do, and as a result, they both received the blessings of God. Notice that when God called Abraham, he chose to obey God by faith, even though he did not know where the path would lead. His faith and trust were in the sovereign hand of the Lord. As a result of following God, Abraham received a blessing—an inheritance.

What do we learn in Galatians 3:8?

_____

_____

Just like our Old Testament overcomers Noah and Abraham, we need to put our faith and trust in God even when our circumstances don't make sense. We must keep our eyes fixed on the Lord and on His great promises for us.

To be an overcomer, we must have faith.

Fill in the blanks below for Hebrews 11:1-3 (ESV):

Now _____ is the assurance of things hoped for, the conviction of things not seen. For by it the people of old received their commendation. By _____ we understand that the universe was created by the word of God, so that what is seen was not made out of things that are visible.

What can we learn about faith in the following verses?

Matthew 17:20

_____

_____

Matthew 21:21-22

_____

_____

Romans 1:17

_____

_____

Ephesians 2:8

_____

_____

Let's read Hebrews 11:6,

> "And without faith it is impossible to please God, because anyone who comes to him must believe that he exists and that he rewards those who earnestly seek him" (NIV).

With faith, nothing is impossible. The righteous children of God live by faith. It is by the grace of

God that we have been saved, rather than through our own works.

Salvation has confounded men through the ages. We want to earn God's favor but can't do a single thing to earn His grace—and there is nothing we *can* do. It is a precious gift from God, freely given.

He didn't wait for us to become holy. Instead, while we were yet sinners, he endured the cross so that we could be reconciled to God. God needs nothing from us but, because He loves us, He desires our heart and pursues a relationship with us. God is our loving Father and we are his children.

Write out 1 Peter 1:3-9 in the lines provided below.

_____
_____
_____
_____
_____
_____
_____
_____
_____
_____
_____
_____
_____

The Message translates 1 Peter 1:3-9 beautifully:

> What a God we have! And how fortunate we are to have him, this Father of our Master Jesus! Because Jesus was raised from the dead, we've been given a brand-new life and have everything to live for, including a future in heaven—and the future starts now! God is keeping careful watch over us and the future. The Day is coming when you'll have it all—life healed and whole.
>
> I know how great this makes you feel, even though you have to put up with every kind of aggravation in the meantime. Pure gold put in the fire comes out of it proved pure; genuine faith put through this suffering comes out proved genuine. When Jesus wraps this all up, it's your faith, not your gold, that God will have on display as evidence of his victory.
>
> You never saw him, yet you love him. You still don't see him, yet you trust him—with laughter and singing. Because you kept on believing, you'll get what you're looking forward to: total salvation.

Sanctification

While we are here on earth, we will experience hardship, but God will use all of our troubles for our sanctification. Through that process, He will conform us into His image, to be used as instruments for His good will. We are His chosen vessels and we have been born again into living hope.

According to *Baker's Evangelical Dictionary of Biblical Theology*, the general meaning of sanctification is "the state of proper functioning."[2]

To sanctify someone or something is to set that person or thing apart for the use intended by its designer. For instance, I use my dishwasher to wash dishes, my kitchen mixer to combine ingredients and mix things together, and my kitchen knives to cut things. I don't put things in the dishwasher to combine them or place dishes in my mixer in the hope that they will come clean. I don't try to eat with a knife. Each of my kitchen appliances and utensils were designed to fulfill a distinct purpose, and when properly used, they are "sanctified" to fulfill a specific role. As people of God, we are sanctified when we do what God intends for us to do. God has a specific plan for our lives, and when we function as He intends, we fulfill God's purpose and design.

The Greek word translated from "sanctification" (hagiasmos [aJgiasmov"]) means "holiness." To sanctify, therefore, means "to make holy."

In this life, we will be tested with trials of all kinds, but it is through this testing that our faith is proven. By faith, we believe in Jesus, even though we cannot see Him. We believe in what He has done for us. We understand that it is because of His great sacrifice that we are saved, and that anyone who is born of God will overcome the world.

By faith, we must look to the Jesus we can't see, not our circumstances that we can see. Our circumstances do not define us; instead, our identity is found in Christ.

Declarations

By grace, I have been saved through faith.

With faith, *nothing* is impossible.

I have an inheritance that is imperishable, undefiled, and unfading.

My trials test the genuineness of my faith and make me more like Christ.

Overcoming in Your Life

What is God teaching you about faith today?

_____

_____

What steps of obedience can you take in faith today?

_____

_____

 Prayer

Increase our faith, Lord, and help us to trust You more each day! Help us to be more like Abraham and walk by faith. Let us keep our eyes fixed on you, even when everything around us in this world doesn't make sense. In those moments, help us to have eyes of faith to see. Lord, lead us, guide us, and direct us in our path. Let Your kingdom come and Your will be done here on earth, just as it is in heaven. In Jesus's precious and mighty name, we pray.

DAY 3

Integrity is doing the right thing when you don't have to—when no one else is looking or will ever know—when there will be no congratulations or recognition for having done so. —Charles Marshall[3]

Moving through our review of the Old Testament, we continue on to read about the descendants of Abraham, including his sons Isaac and Jacob.

In Genesis 37, we learn about Jacob's descendants. Jacob had many sons but loved his son Joseph more than any of the others. As a token of his affection, he even gave him a coat of many colors. Joseph's brothers knew he was his father's beloved son, and it sparked jealousy and hatred among them. Their feelings were amplified even more when Joseph shared the dreams he had with his family about how his brothers would bow to his rule. As a result, his brothers plotted against Joseph, and some even wanted him dead. Finally, they decided not to kill him, but to throw him into a pit instead. He remained in the pit until some traders passed by, and his brothers sold him to the traders into slavery. After becoming a slave, he was taken to Egypt.

Joseph's story begins as a promising dream, but the dream quickly turns into a nightmare. He goes from being the favored son to the pit, and from the pit into slavery. Yet through it all, the Lord was with him and blessed him despite his circumstances.

We pick up the story again in Genesis 39, where it tells us the story of what happens to Joseph once he arrives in Egypt.

Read Genesis 39:2-3.

Who was with Joseph?

_____

What happened as a result?

_____

_____

The Lord's favor remained with Joseph, and he became a successful man who lived in the house of his Egyptian master. His master saw that the Lord was with him and that, as a result, he succeeded in all he did. Though he began his time in Egypt as a slave, Joseph was eventually elevated to a position of authority in his master Potiphar's house.

Let's pick up our story in Genesis 39:6-10:

> So he left all that he had in Joseph's charge, and because of him he had no concern about anything but the food he ate. Now Joseph was handsome in form and appearance. And after a time his master's wife cast her eyes on Joseph and said, "Lie with me." But he refused and said to his master's wife, "Behold, because of me my master has no concern about anything in the house, and he has put everything that he has in my charge. He is not greater in this house than I am, nor has he kept back anything from me except you, because you are his wife. How then can I do this great wickedness and sin against God?" And as she spoke to Joseph day after day, he would not listen to her, to lie beside her or to be with her.

Joseph was a good-looking guy, and the Lord blessed him with a position of authority. Potiphar's wife tempted him to lie with her, but he refused because he was a man of integrity.

When Joseph refuses temptation, who does he say the sin would be against?

_____

_____

When you are tempted to sin, do you consider that sin is wickedness before the Lord?

_____

_____

Again, Joseph is tempted by Potiphar's wife, but this time she accuses him of betrayal. He is punished by being sent to prison. At that point, his circumstances must have seemed pretty bleak. I wonder if he questioned whether or not the Lord had forgotten about him.

Why would a good and loving God allow Joseph to endure such hardship in the midst of his faithfulness?

Read Genesis 39:21-23.

What do you learn from these verses?

_____

_____

These verses seem just as applicable to us today as they were to Joseph when he was imprisoned in Egypt. Despite Joseph's circumstances, he prospered, even while in prison. The Lord was with Joseph and loved him. As a result, he was blessed. Regardless of the circumstances that we find ourselves in today, we can count on the fact that God loves us and will never leave us.

Read Hebrews 13:5-6.

What comfort do these verses provide?

_____

_____

If you are a child of God, His Spirit resides within you, and you are never alone.

Beloved, He will never leave us nor forsake us. No matter where the twists and turns on the path of life may take us, whether we are in a pit or a palace, God holds us within the palm of his mighty hand.

Declarations

I will have integrity and strive to always do the right thing.

Lord, regardless of my circumstances, I trust you with my life.

When all hope seems lost, I will hold firm to my faith and praise you.

I am never alone. God is always with me.

Overcoming in Your Life

We can do all the right things and still end up in places we have never imagined. God wants our obedience and our praise regardless of our circumstances.

Where has God positioned you today to be a faithful witness?

_____

_____

Ask God how you can better love and serve those around you in your current season of life. Record any insights.

_____

_____

Has your life taken unexpected twists and turns? Praise God that He sees the entire tapestry when we can only see the messy threads!

moses

DAY 4

Faith showeth us that God loveth us, that he forgiveth us our sins, that He accounteth us for His children having freely justified us through the blood of His son. —John Bunyan[4]

Continuing on our journey through the Old Testament, let's fast-forward through the next four books of the Bible: Exodus, Leviticus, Numbers, and Deuteronomy. It is in those books where we meet our next overcomer, Moses. Moses was born in Egypt as a Hebrew at the time when the pharaoh of Egypt had ordered all male Hebrew babies be killed. To avoid this fate, Moses's mother hid him in a basket of made of reeds and placed him in the river. He was found by pharaoh's daughter and was raised in the Egyptian palace as a member of the royal family.

As Moses matured, he began to notice the plight of his people–the Israelite slaves– and turned his back on the royal family. After an altercation with an Egyptian, he fled to Midian, where an angel of the Lord appeared to him in a burning bush (Exodus 2). At that point, God told Moses to go back to Egypt and lead the Israelites out of slavery, through the Red Sea, and into the promised land.

Let's read Hebrews 11:23-29 to see what it has to say about Moses. Underline the repeated phrase.

> By faith Moses, when he was born, was hidden for three months by his parents, because they saw that the child was beautiful, and they were not afraid of the king's edict. By faith Moses, when he was grown up, refused to be called the son of Pharaoh's daughter, choosing rather to be mistreated with the people of God than to enjoy the fleeting pleasures of sin. He considered the reproach of Christ greater wealth than the treasures of Egypt, for he was looking to the reward. By faith he left Egypt, not being afraid of the anger of the king, for he endured as seeing him who is invisible. By faith he kept the Passover and sprinkled the blood, so that the Destroyer of the firstborn might not touch them. By faith the people crossed the Red Sea as on dry land, but the Egyptians, when they attempted to do the same, were drowned.

Did you see the repeated phrase, "by faith"? Underline, circle, or highlight each time you see the word faith. The phrase "by faith" is used five times in this passage. Anything that we see repeated in scripture should get our attention. Throughout this passage, we learn that it was by faith that Moses obeyed God. Even though Moses did not feel equipped to lead the Israelites out of their enslavement, he stepped out in faith and followed the Lord, much like Abraham and Noah.

Power in Overcoming

Moses led the Israelites out of Egypt, where they wandered in the wilderness for forty years. Finally, they arrived at the edge of the promised land, but before they entered, Moses sent twelve spies to decide how best to conquer the land and its inhabitants. This is where we find the first use of the word "overcome," in Numbers 13:30, "But Caleb quieted the people before Moses and said, "Let us go up at once and occupy it, for we are well able to overcome it." (ESV).

The word "overcome," in the original Hebrew, according to *Strong's Concordance*, is the transliteration *yakol*. Transliteration means to take the letters from one ל כ.י , text and translate them to another. The Hebrew transliteration *yakol* means "to be able" or "to have power." This gives us more insight into what it means to overcome.

If we overcome, we are able, and we have power.

As Joshua 1:8-9 says,

> This Book of the Law shall not depart from your mouth, but you shall meditate on it day and night, so that you may be careful to do according to all that is written in it. For then you will make your way prosperous, and then you will have good success. Have I not commanded you? Be strong and courageous. Do not be frightened, and do not be dismayed, for the Lord your God is with you wherever you go.

We are not supposed to be afraid; instead, we are to be strong and courageous because God is with us.

Write out the following verses.

2 Timothy 1:7

_____

_____

Exodus 14:14

_____

_____

Philippians 4:13

_____

_____

Aren't you glad that God is always with us?

We do not need to be afraid; fear is the opposite of faith.

The Lord has commanded us to not be afraid. We do not need to be afraid because the Lord is with us and will fight for us. He has given us a spirit of power and love.

Declarations

God gave me a spirit of power, love, and self-control.

God will fight for me.

Because of the power of Christ that lives in me, *I can do all things.*

Overcoming in Your Life

When you feel alone or afraid, God is only a breath away. Call upon the name of Lord. Cry out to Him in your time of need and begin to praise Him!

_____

_____

I have a friend whose favorite slogan is "Do it afraid!" How can you take baby steps in faith today?

_____

_____

Believe that you can do all things through Christ and remind yourself that it is through His power and strength that you can accomplish His will

daniel and job

DAY 5

If you fell down yesterday, stand up today. —H. G. Wells[5]

We have reached our final day of studying overcomers in the Old Testament this week, and that leads us to our final two. We begin today's lesson with Daniel. Daniel and his companions serve as an excellent example of what it means to be an overcomer. The book of Daniel begins with Daniel being taken Babylon. In Daniel 1:1 we are told, "In the third year of the reign of Jehoiakim king of Judah, Nebuchadnezzar king of Babylon came to Jerusalem and besieged it." Along with the seizure of some of the vessels of the House of God, some of the people—including Daniel—were taken into captivity.

Begin by reading Daniel 1:1-21.

In these verses, we learn that Daniel was highly favored by the king. By faith, he also withstood many trials and temptations.

Daniel 1:8 says, "But Daniel resolved that he would not defile himself with the king's food, or with the wine that he drank. Therefore he asked the chief of the eunuchs to allow him not to defile himself."

The New Living Translation says it this way:

"Daniel was determined not to defile himself."

Put another way, the New American Standard Bible says that "Daniel made up his mind."

What is the very first thing Daniel did? Daniel *resolved*, he was *determined*, and he *made up his mind* that he would not be defiled. According to *Merriam-Webster*, the definition of "resolve" is "to make a definite and serious decision to do something."[6]

Daniel was taken in captivity to Babylon, yet he remained resolved to not defile himself with the king's food or wine while living in a foreign land. Daniel chose to live a life of integrity rather than submit to the popular culture of his time. He made a stand for what was right and, as a result of his faithfulness, God blessed him.

Just like Daniel, the enemy would love to see us enslaved by food and drink. But this is not his only trick—the enemy also wants to carry us into captivity in our minds by convincing us that we are not good enough, that somehow, we have sinned too much, or that we have so ruined our lives that we could never be used by God. These are lies straight from the pit of hell.

Dating Advice For My Son

When my son was a young man and became interested in pursuing the affections of a young lady, we had many talks about purity and God's design for marriage. I knew that I could teach my son what was right and what was wrong, but I also knew it was up to him to follow through. So before he began dating, I told him he needed to make his mind up before he ever went on a date what his boundary was going to be. Would he hold hands? Would he kiss?

He needed to determine beforehand what his boundary would be rather than waiting until the heat of the moment on a date. He needed to resolve his boundary long before he was ever alone with a girl.

Are there areas of your life where God has called you to be resolved? Take a moment to reflect quietly and jot down your thoughts.

_____
_____
_____

The Overcomer's Secret

In my research for this study, I found a tiny little booklet amongst the thousands of books in the theological library. The booklet was called *The Overcomer's Secret – Studies in the Book of Daniel*, by Bakht Singh. This booklet is packed full of wisdom, as Singh details Daniel and the lessons we can learn from him. Singh writes,

> God brought Daniel into high favor with the king and the king gave him unprecedented power in the Empire. In the same way God is raising up a company of people called overcomers. They have to bear great trials, and painful burdens, but God is planning to bring them finally into great favor in His Kingdom and to give them much more than any man can expect or imagine.[7]

Did you hear that truth? God wants us all to be overcomers! Bakht Singh provides further encouragement for overcomers in his analysis of Daniel and his friends' example: "What a great, eternal spiritual and glorious inheritance is being prepared in heaven for those who overcome . . . Like these young men we also may have to go through refining fires, but all these sufferings will help us to become overcomers. Eventually we will become more than conquerors in everything."[8]

Daniel resolved not to be defiled by the prevailing winds of culture. He stood firm in that decision and continued to be faithful to the Lord, all the way to the lion's den. Despite outside pressure, Daniel continued to do what was right in the eyes of God, not man. He knew his God was able to save him!

Job as an Overcomer

We move on now to perhaps the most iconic overcomer of the Old Testament, Job. Job endured many trials.

Let's begin our study by reading the first chapter in the book of Job:

Job's Character and Wealth

There was a man in the land of Uz whose name was Job, and that man was blameless and upright, one who feared God and turned away from evil. There were born to him seven sons and three daughters. He possessed 7,000 sheep, 3,000 camels, 500 yoke of oxen, and 500 female donkeys, and very many servants, so that this man was the greatest of all the people of the east. His sons used to go and hold a feast in the house of each one on his day, and they would send and invite their three sisters to eat and drink with them. And when the days of the feast had run their course, Job would send and consecrate them, and he would rise early in the morning and offer burnt offerings according to the number of them all. For Job said, "It may be that my children have sinned, and cursed God in their hearts." Thus Job did continually.

Satan Allowed to Test Job

Now there was a day when the sons of God came to present themselves before the Lord, and Satan also came among them. The Lord said to Satan, "From where have you come?" Satan answered the Lord and said, "From going to and fro on the earth, and from walking up and down on it." And the Lord said to Satan, "Have you considered my servant Job, that there is none like him on the earth, a blameless and upright man, who fears God and turns away from evil?" Then Satan answered the Lord and said, "Does Job fear God for no reason? Have you not put a hedge around him and his house and all that he has, on every side? You have blessed the work of his hands, and his possessions have increased in the land. But stretch out your hand and touch all that he has, and he will curse you to your face." And the Lord said to Satan, "Behold, all that he has is in your hand. Only against him do not stretch out your hand." So Satan went out from the presence of the Lord.

Satan Takes Job's Property and Children

Now there was a day when his sons and daughters were eating and drinking wine in their oldest brother's house, and there came a messenger to Job and said, "The oxen were plowing and the donkeys feeding beside them, and the Sabeans fell upon them and took them and struck down the servants with the edge of the sword, and I alone have escaped to tell you." While he was yet speaking, there came another and said, "The fire of God fell from heaven and burned up the sheep and the servants and consumed them, and I alone have escaped to tell you." While he was yet speaking, there came another and said, "The Chaldeans formed three groups and made a raid on the camels and took them and struck down the servants with the edge of the sword, and I alone have escaped to tell you." While he was yet speaking, there came another and said, "Your sons and daughters were eating and drinking wine in their oldest brother's house, and behold, a great wind came across the wilderness and struck the four corners of the house, and it fell upon the young people, and they are dead, and I alone have escaped to tell you."

Then Job arose and tore his robe and shaved his head and fell on the ground and worshiped. And he said, "Naked I came from my mother's womb, and naked shall I return. The Lord gave, and the Lord has taken away; blessed be the name of the Lord." In all this Job did not sin or charge God with wrong.

Job was a man of great wealth and other blessings, but neither of those attributes are highlighted first in his description. Instead, what is the first thing we learn about Job after his name and location?

_____

_____

It's significant that the first thing we learn about Job is his noble character. Job fears the Lord. He is considered blameless and upright, someone who turns away from evil.

In the subsequent verses in Job 1, we learn that Satan was allowed to test Job. Satan begins by taking away Job's property and children, then attacks his health. Although Job laments his losses, he remains faithful in the midst of his circumstances. Despite the counsel of four of his friends, Job remains loyal to God.

The book of Job comes to a climax in chapter 38, when God speaks to Job and challenges him. It concludes with Job's confession and repentance, as Job humbles himself before the Lord and finds his life and fortunes restored.

In fact, Job is blessed in even greater measure than ever before.

As Job 42:12 says, "The Lord blessed the latter days of Job more than his beginning.

Declarations

I am highly favored.

I stand resolved not to be defiled by the prevailing winds of culture.

By faith, I will overcome trials and temptations.

I stand resolved to do what is right in the sight of the Lord.

Overcoming in Your Life

Humbling, isn't it? Aren't you glad that God wants us all to be overcomers?

_____

_____

What does integrity look like in your life?

_____

_____

Write out a prayer of thanksgiving to God. No matter what circumstances come our way, let's choose to remain faithful, live in humility, and pursue a life marked by integrity.

_____

_____

 Prayer

Lord, help us resolve in our hearts not to be defiled by sin. Help us to follow you no matter where the path of life takes us and regardless of whatever circumstance comes our way. Help us to keep our eyes fixed only on you, Lord! Make us overcomers like Daniel, Job, and others who sought after you in the Old Testament!

Well done, friends! We are halfway through our study on what it means to be an overcomer.

We have spent the past three weeks laying a foundation by following the thread of overcoming throughout the Old Testament. Next week, we will spring forward to the New Testament and look at Jesus, the Overcomer!

Week 4

JESUS, THE ANSWER AND ULTIMATE OVERCOMER

DAY 1

"You stir man to take pleasure in praising you, because you have made us for yourself, and our heart is restless until it rests in you."—Augustine of Hippo, *Confessions*[1]

Everything we have studied so far has laid the groundwork for this week.

Beginning today, we will concentrate on our promised King, Jesus Christ—the ultimate overcomer. He was the one who dealt with our sin problem on the cross at Calvary and redeemed us. Jesus is spectacular; He truly is everything! He is the answer to all of the struggles and problems presented in the previous chapters, and it is our faith in Him that empowers us to be more than conquerors.

On our first day of study together, we briefly looked at John 1:1-5. Today I would like to dive a little deeper into the text.

Read John 1:1-18 and take note of anything that stands out to you.

_____
_____
_____
_____
_____

What is the first thing we learn from these verses?

_____
_____

Where was Jesus in the beginning?

_____

What was made through Him?

_____

What is in Jesus?

_____

The word of God became flesh in the person of Jesus. God humbled Himself and took on human form; Jesus was fully God and fully man. The verses in John 1:14-18 focus on his deity.

John MacArthur, in the *MacArthur Bible Commentary*, says, "The infinite became finite. The eternal was conformed to time. The invisible became visible. The supernatural One reduced Himself to the natural."[2]

Isn't that amazing! God did not cease being God, but through Jesus, humbled Himself and took on human form. He left heaven in order to come to earth and dwell among us.

The Light of the World

In Jesus, there is life, and that life is full of light. The bright light of Jesus shines in the darkness and is the light of men. The darkness cannot overcome it. Instead, Jesus overcomes darkness! John came to bear witness to Jesus that all who believed might be saved.

The gospel is the good news; it is the best story that has ever been told! Jesus was present in the world and came to give His light to everyone. Unfortunately, the world didn't know Him; even His people did not receive him—instead, they rejected Him.

Despite being rejected, Jesus's continued message of faith in Him and acceptance of His sacrifice for our sins on the cross have forever changed our relationship with Him. Now, all who believe in Him can become children of God. When we put our faith and trust in Jesus Christ, not only are we called children of God, but we have access to His power to overcome the world.

God promised us a king that would redeem us to himself. Because of His love for us, He sent His son to penetrate the darkness and overcome the world!

Begin today by reading Hebrews 1:1-4. In the Old Testament, God spoke to our forefathers through the prophets. How has He chosen to speak to us in the last days?

_____

What does this choice say about His nature?

_____

_____

Who does Jesus outrank, according to Hebrews 1:4?

_____

What does Colossians 2:9 say about Jesus?

_____

_____

What does Colossians 1:19 tell us?

_____

_____

The Supremacy of Christ

These scriptures tell us that Jesus is God. Jesus is the ultimate supreme being.

Merriam-Webster Dictionary defines "supreme" as "highest in rank or authority" or "highest in degree or quality."[3]

It is important for us to understand the supremacy of Christ because there are some religions that try to add or alter the revelation found in the Bible. For instance, some religions believe Jesus was a good man, but not the Savior. As Christians, we believe that Jesus is our Savior and the fulfillment of Old Testament law and prophecy.

Scripture is clear that God speaks to us through Jesus. God spoke to us through the prophets in the Old Testament, but in the last days—our current time—He speaks to us through His son. Jesus is imbued with the radiance of the glory of God and the exact imprint of his nature. In essence, he is a carbon copy of God (being fully God himself), yet in human form. Jesus *is* the final revelation. No other prophet or man can add any other revelation.

God appointed Jesus as the heir of all things. He provides the last word.

Who lays the foundation in 1 Corinthians 3:11?

_____
_____
_____

Read Hebrews 4:15. What do we learn about Jesus being our high priest?

_____
_____
_____

Why is this important?

_____
_____
_____

According to Hebrews 2:18, who is our helper?

_____
_____
_____

What else do we learn about our high priest in Hebrews 7:26?

_____
_____

Fully Man, Fully God

It was important that Jesus was fully man in order to identify with our humanity and sympathize with our frailty. This was not for His sake, but for our sake. While he was on earth, Jesus was tempted. He understood our struggles because He took on flesh and experienced temptation yet remained without sin.

Not only was Jesus fully man, He was also fully God. It is important for us to recognize that Jesus was fully God. Let's look at the following scriptures to see what more we can learn about Jesus.

What do we learn about Jesus in John 14:11?

_____
_____

Read John 8:28. On whose authority does Jesus speak ?

_____
_____

What does John 10:30 tell us?

_____
_____

Read Matthew 1:20. How do we know that Jesus did not inherit Adam's sin nature?

_____
_____

What do we learn about Jesus in Romans 1:1-4?

_____
_____

What does 2 Corinthians 5:21 tell us?

_____

_____

What do we learn about life and death in 2 Timothy 1:10?

_____

_____

What do we learn about Jesus in Colossians 1:15?

_____

Aren't you thankful that Jesus is fully God and fully man?

There is truly no other like Jesus!

Rather than simply being a good teacher or prophet, as some may claim, Jesus embodies the true nature of God.

Jesus is the only begotten son of God. He is God incarnate.

Declarations

Jesus is the answer to all of my problems.

Jesus is fully God and fully man.

Through Jesus Christ, I have the power to overcome!

Overcoming in Your Life

What hope do we have because Jesus humbled himself to take on human form?

_____

_____

Let's close our time today in praise to God. Let's thank him for sending Jesus to not only save us but to understand our human plight. Praise Jesus for His love for us, His humility, and His sacrifice on the cross so we might be saved.

_____

_____

_____

_____

_____

_____

the way of the cross

DAY 2

The way to the crown is the cross. –Robert Murray M'cheyne[4]

You may think that when you become a Christian all of your problems are solved. Perhaps you think that it is like winning the lottery and life will become easy, allowing you to coast through difficulties. This couldn't be further from the truth! Yes, there are blessings for those who are in Christ, and we will consider that later. For now, recognize that Christians face the same problems as unbelievers.

The difference between believers and unbelievers is in our response to our problems and circumstances.

Let's look at what Jesus says about following him in Matthew 16:24. What does Jesus tell the disciples they must do to follow him?

_____

_____

Jesus says, "deny yourself" and "take up your cross and follow me." He doesn't say "follow me; life will be easy, and you will find everything you have ever wanted." Jesus came to earth not as a king, but as a servant who came to bear the sins of the world.

Worthy of the Call

In Matthew 10, when Jesus calls the twelve disciples and sends them out into the world to proclaim the good news, He warns them that persecution will come. In Matthew 10:38, what does Jesus say about taking up the cross?

_____

_____

What do we learn about being a disciple of Jesus in Luke 14:27?

_____

_____

To be considered worthy of being a true disciple of Jesus Christ, you must be willing to deny yourself. In order to deny yourself, you must lay aside your feelings, desires, wishes, and will, and lay them all at the feet of the cross of Jesus Christ in complete surrender. When we surrender ourselves to the cross of Christ and pick up own our cross, we identify ourselves with the suffering of Jesus, His death, and His resurrection. As we die to self, our identity becomes more and more Christlike.

Surrender, Pray, Repeat

What does it mean to "take up your cross"? I think of it as a continuous cycle of surrender, pray, repeat. The cross is a symbol that serves as a reminder of our willingness to die to self and surrender to Jesus. Dying to self is a daily practice. Each morning when we wake up we have a choice: Whom will we serve, God or ourselves?

We cast our cares on Him by giving our burdens and struggles to Jesus through prayer. We can begin by continually praying about our burdens—a million times if necessary—until we can release them to Him. We put our faith and trust in Him, knowing that He will help us get through our battles.

Practice a daily habit of surrender, pray, repeat.

We surrender ourselves to Jesus and pray about our problems.

Jesus is All We Need

It is our natural inclination to want to share our problems with our friends. Although there is wisdom in seeking godly counsel, Jesus is the friend we should turn to first.

When my own life has felt overwhelming at times, I have sought the counsel of my friends. Sometimes, I wouldn't even ask for help, I would simply complain about my problems. Oftentimes, praying was something that happened only after I asked my friends for advice. Unfortunately, praying was an afterthought instead of my first thought. God wants to be our comforter and share in our burdens. In exchange, He gives us peace.

Jesus is the friend we should turn to first.

We live in a broken and messy world. Other people, problems, and sin can all cause us to have anxiety and rob us of our joy. Over and over in the Psalms, we see that God is described as our refuge, our fortress, and our strength. The book of Psalms is a great place to go for comfort when we are feeling overwhelmed with our circumstances. As we mediate on the Psalms, we will often find peace and comfort.

Here's a great example: "The Lord is my rock and my fortress and my deliverer, my God, my rock, in whom I take refuge, my shield, and the horn of my salvation, my stronghold," (Psalm 18:2).

Following Jesus

We are to seek the will of God and follow Christ no matter the cost. As Christ's followers, we must deny ourselves and follow Him—after all, we are told that whomever does not deny himself, cannot be His disciple.
Lord, help us to follow You with all our hearts! Teach us how to deny ourselves and surrender to Your will so that we may follow You all the days of our lives.

Remember the Greek meaning of overcomer, *nike*. The original meaning illustrates how, as Christians, we are to be overcomers. If we are to overcome, then there must be something that we must conquer in order to live victoriously.

D. L. Moody, in his book *The Overcoming Life*, explains the consequence of following Christ, "The Christian life is a conflict and a warfare, and the quicker we find it out, the better."[5] If we are to live a victorious Christian life, then we must be engaged in battle.

What Does Victory Look Like?

Look up Proverbs 3:5-6. What are we called to do?

_____
_____
_____

What will the Lord do for us if we follow that call?

_____
_____

Life can be chaotic at times. In Psalm 55:22, what are we told to do with our cares?

_____
_____

I like the way Psalm 55:22 is phrased in the New Living Translation,

> "Give your burdens to the LORD, and he will take care of you. He will not permit the godly to slip and fall." The Lord wants to be our refuge and shelter. He wants us to give Him our troubles and burdens.

Over and over in the Psalms, we see God described as our refuge, our fortress, and our strength. What do we learn from the following verses?

Psalm 46:1-3

_____
_____

Psalm 91:2

_____
_____

The Lord is our helper and gives us strength. When trouble comes, He is our refuge and fortress from the storms of life. Reliance on God is easier to say than it is to do sometimes; the struggle really is real. Thankfully, the presence of God is just as real. He is only a breath of prayer away.

Let's look at two more scriptures to see what we can do when difficult circumstances arise.

In 1 Peter 5:7, what are we told to do with anxiety?

_____
_____

What does Jesus tell us to do in Matthew 11:28-30?

_____
_____

Declarations

God, I trust in You to guide me, lead me, and direct me.

Lord, You are my helper. When I cast my cares on You, You strengthen me.

Heavenly Father, I surrender my will to Yours. I choose today to pick up my cross and follow You.

Overcoming in Your Life

What is God calling you to lay at the foot of the cross today?

_____
_____
_____
_____
_____

Is there an area of your life where you need to deny yourself and surrender to Him?

_____
_____
_____
_____

Do you journal? Journaling is a great way to record both your prayers and God's answers to those prayers. It is a fantastic way to trace the faithfulness of God in your life and can serve as a powerful reminder of God's unchanging favor when times are tough.

I began journaling my prayers early in my marriage, and I now have stacks of journals full of my cries to the Lord. They are a record of His faithfulness! I also use my journals to write out passages of scripture on which I can meditate. There is something about the act of hand writing a verse that helps you commit it to memory. If you don't already have a prayer journal, consider starting one to help capture your thoughts and prayers.

Conclude today's lesson by journaling your heart to the Lord.

_____
_____
_____
_____
_____
_____
_____
_____
_____
_____

Jesus overcomes the world

DAY 3

When you suffer and lose that does not mean you are being disobedient to God. In fact, it might mean you're right in the center of his will. The path of obedience is often marked by times of suffering and loss. —Chuck Swindoll[6]

The Christian life is filled with trials and tribulations. We all face adversity at some point in our lives. When difficulties come our way, we have a choice to make on how we respond: We can choose to succumb and become bitter, or we can embrace those trials and let them make us better.

The final discourse of Jesus is given in John 13:31-16:33.

Jesus leaves his disciples with a final word of encouragement. In doing so, Jesus tells his disciples one of the most important things that we need to know for this study. Look up John 16:33 and write it below.

_____
_____
_____

In this verse, Jesus warns his disciples that they will face trials and tribulations. Christ came to give both his disciples and us peace, joy, and victory over the world.

According to 1 Corinthians 15:57, from where does our victory come?

_____

We do not overcome the world. The word "I" in that sentence is very emphatic, and it refers to Jesus. Jesus has overcome the world. Through Jesus's death, burial, and resurrection we are no longer alienated from a holy, just, and righteous God. Jesus defeated Satan through the power of the cross so that we can have communion with God.

What does Jesus say that we should have in John 16:33?

_____
_____

Finding Peace

Everywhere we go today, people are stressed. Is that the way we are supposed to live? Are we to be filled with anxiety and allow stress to overtake our lives? No! We are to have peace and, through Jesus Christ, we can experience His perfect peace.

What do we learn from Philippians 4:4-7? Write these verses below.

_____

_____

_____

_____

_____

Now read Philippians 4:4-7 in The Message Bible:

> Celebrate God all day, every day. I mean, revel in him! Make it as clear as you can to all you meet that you're on their side, working with them and not against them. Help them see that the Master is about to arrive. He could show up any minute!

> Don't fret or worry. Instead of worrying, pray. Let petitions and praises shape your worries into prayers, letting God know your concerns. Before you know it, a sense of God's wholeness, everything coming together for good, will come and settle you down. It's wonderful what happens when Christ displaces worry at the center of your life.

Celebrate God and revel in Him daily.

What a beautiful concept! We get to exchange the burdens and cares of this world with the peace of Christ. Through our prayer and our praise, we can be at peace with the challenges we face in life, as long as we abide in Jesus Christ. We do not need to be anxious about anything at all. We are to pray with thanksgiving and praise and, in return, He gives us peace that passes all understanding. This peace guards our heart and our mind. We won't find this peace anywhere else in the world; it comes only from Jesus.

Is it possible for us to always be at peace? Does God want us to be at peace when we lose our job? How about when someone we love is sick? How can we maintain our faith when we lose loved one? There is no easy solution to these difficulties, but as we abide in Jesus Christ, we can have peace regardless of our circumstances.

Look up the following verses and record what you learn about peace.

Colossians 3:15

_____

_____

Proverbs 12:20

_____

_____

Psalm 29:11

_____

_____

Psalm 119:165

_____

_____

Isaiah 26:3

_____

_____

When we abide in Christ, we can exchange the heartache and cares of this world for the peace of God. Even in the midst of difficult circumstances, it is possible to have peace. Jesus is the Prince of Peace. If you are carrying the weight of the world with you today, or possess a burdensome heaviness in your circumstances, I encourage you to stop and ask God to take away your burden and exchange it for His peace.

_____

_____

_____

Sometimes our blessings come through tears and hardship. It's when we are broken and at the end of ourselves that we are able to see our great need for God. It is often when we are at our lowest that He can do His greatest work in and through us.

Our Hope Is in Jesus

Wherever we are on the road of life, we can cling to the truth of Romans 5:8.

What comfort does this verse provide?

_____

_____

Jesus came to save us. The Lord loves us; we are his creation and he wants a relationship with us. I'm so glad that even in the midst of our sin, Jesus chose to redeem us! He wants to restore our broken relationship with the Father, caused by our sin, into wholeness.

Read Deuteronomy 31:6. How has God demonstrated this concept in your life?

_____

_____

In this verse, Moses assures Joshua and the Israelites that God's presence is a promise. The same God that was with the Israelites yesterday is the same God that is with us today and will be forever. We can cling to the truth that we, too, can be strong and courageous! According to _Benson's Commentary_, "This promise though made at this time particularly to Israel and Joshua, yet belongs to all believers."[7] We are not to be frightened, dismayed, or discouraged. The Lord our God is with us wherever we go. God's presence surrounds us.

Look up Acts 2:21 and Romans 10:13. Who will the Lord save, according to these verses?

_____

_____

Declarations

Jesus has overcome the world. Through Him, we also have victory to overcome!

The Lord strengthens me and gives me peace. The peace of Jesus Christ rules in my heart.

I don't have to be afraid because God is always near.

Overcoming in Your Life

When trials come your way, what do you do? How do you respond?

_____
_____
_____

Are you willing to praise God no matter what circumstances arise?

_____
_____
_____

 Prayer

Jesus, we are so thankful that You calm the storms in our life. Help us to be able to praise You in the storm. Give us peace when we are struggling, Lord. Help us to walk through adversity, knowing You are there with us. Guide us, direct us, and comfort us. Strengthen us for battle as we cling to You. Amen.

surrendered to Jesus

DAY 4

My son, give me your heart, and let your eyes observe my ways. —Proverbs 23:26

Begin today's study by looking at Romans 12:21 and filling in the blanks: Do not be _____ by evil, but _____ evil with good.

In this verse, we see the word overcome used twice. In the original language, the first word used is *niko*—"do not be overcome by evil"—and the second time it is *nika*—"overcome evil." Paul presents us with two options—either we overcome evil, or evil will overcome us.

In the Christian life, we are to love one another, forgive one another, and bless one another. It is through these "one anothers" of scripture that we will overcome evil. Unforgiveness only harms us.

What does Ephesians 4:32 tell us about how we are to act and why?
_____
_____

Turn to Galatians 2:20. What does Paul tell us in this verse? Who lives in Paul?
_____

How does this impact the way Paul lives?
_____
_____

Obedience by Faith

In this study, we have already learned so much about what it means to be an overcomer. I am excited about what we are going to learn today.

Read 1 John 5:1-5:

> Everyone who believes that Jesus is the Christ has been born of God, and everyone who loves the Father loves whoever has been born of him. By this we know that we love the children of God, when we love God and obey his commandments. For this is the love of God, that we keep his commandments. And his commandments are not burdensome. For everyone who has been born of God overcomes the world. And this is the victory that has overcome the world—our faith. Who is it that overcomes the world except the one who believes that Jesus is the Son of God?

From this passage, what do we learn about everyone who believes in Jesus?

_____

_____

How is our love known?

_____

_____

Who overcomes the world in these verses?

_____

_____

What is the victory that has overcome the world?

_____

_____

Wow! Did you read that truth? Because of the sacrifice of Jesus Christ on the cross at Calvary, not only does He overcome the world, but everyone who believes in Him overcomes the world, too!

Our faith in Jesus Christ overcomes the world.

This is true not only at the moment we believe in Jesus, but as an ongoing action of exercising our faith in Jesus that overcomes the world.

Digging Deeper

In his commentary on John 1, Robert S. Candlish says:

> This implies faith; and faith in constant and lively exercise. Our overcoming the world is not an achievement completed at once, and once for all, in our being begotten of God. It is a life long [sic] business, a prolonged and continuous triumph in a prolonged and continuous strife. We are to be always to be new, all our days overcoming the world; "and this is the victory that overcometh the world, even our faith" are being born of God, does indeed give us the victory; it puts us in the right position and endowed us with the needful power for overcoming the world".[8]

Our daily practice of faith is a conscious decision to choose to believe God in good times, in bad times, and all the time. That is what overcomes evil. We don't just believe God once and find that our problems have been magically solved. Rather, it is our continuous, ongoing walk of faith that ensures we overcome. As we have studied, we are both witnesses and participants in the ongoing struggle between good and evil. As such, we must choose every day to put on the full armor of God. As our scripture passage notes and as Candlish details, it is our faith in Christ that ultimately allows us to overcome the world.

Zondervan Exegetical Commentary on the New Testament provides further insight into 1 John 5:4:

> For everything born of God overcomes the world . . . Because Jesus destroyed the works of the devil (3:8) and has overcome the world, those who have been born of God (note the perfect tense) also overcome the world by their faith in Christ. . . . Verse 1 states that Jesus is the Christ has been born of God: v4a, that everything born of God overcomes the world.

Therefore, everyone who believes that Jesus is Christ over-comes the world . . . Without faith in Christ, no one is able to face down the evil, the hopelessness, and the self-defeat that this world presses against us day by day. There are many self-help gurus who write and speak about how to live a better life, and some of what they say may be helpful and worthwhile. But what is of the world cannot give us victory over the world. Without trust in Christ, who came into the world from God, even the most successful life is swallowed up in defeat of death.[9]

The moment we believe that Jesus Christ died on our behalf to save us is the moment we instantly become an overcomer. Without faith in Jesus Christ, we are hopeless and destined to eternal damnation. This is because sin separates us from a Holy God, and it is only through his atoning sacrifice that Jesus provided a way for us to be reconciled to God. Jesus paid the penalty of our sin on the cross, overcoming death and hell on our behalf. It is our faith and trust in Jesus Christ alone that sets us free.

Christ came to overcome the darkness and depravity that has taken hold of this earth. He alone can overcome the sin that has marred God's beautiful creation. We can seek to better ourselves through our own strength, by pulling ourselves up by our bootstraps, or with the help of motivational speaker or self-help books. These people and resources may be helpful to us, but only Jesus can truly change us. Only He can save us.

We are overcomers because we have victory in Jesus

Jesus, the Founder and Perfecter of Our Faith

Read Hebrews 12:1-6:

> Therefore, since we are surrounded by so great a cloud of witnesses, let us also lay aside every weight, and sin which clings so closely, and let us run with endurance the race that is set before us, looking to Jesus, the founder and perfecter of our faith, who for the joy that was set before him endured the cross, despising the shame, and is seated at the right hand of the throne of God. Consider him who endured from sinners such hostility against himself, so that you may not grow weary or fainthearted. In your struggle against sin you have not yet resisted to the point of shedding your blood. And have you forgotten the exhortation that addresses you as sons?

> "My son, do not regard lightly the discipline of the Lord, nor be weary when reproved by him. For the Lord disciplines the one he loves, and chastises every son whom he receives."

Know that there is a crowd cheering us on from heavenly places. These are the saints who have gone on before us.

How are we expected to run the race?

_____

_____

How do we accomplish that aim?

_____

_____

We have received a charge from those who have gone before us to remain faithful and to run with endurance the race set before us. To let go of sin and run with endurance, we need to be properly nourished by the word of God, holding fast to all of the promises in His word.

What does Hebrews 12:2 say about Jesus?

_____

_____

_____

Jesus obediently submitted to death and endured the cross so that we would know Him and could be reconciled to God the Father, our loving creator. God gave us the gift of His son Jesus, the founder and perfecter of our faith. Jesus is now seated in the heavenly realm at the right hand of God, a position of honor.

What hope do we find in Hebrews 12:3?

_____

_____

_____

While on earth, Jesus Christ suffered hostility. When we consider the cross and all that Jesus endured on our behalf, we are encouraged to stay strong in the Lord and not grow weary or fainthearted. The Message Bible illuminates these verses,

> Keep your eyes on Jesus, who both began and finished this race we're in. Study how he did it. Because he never lost sight of where he was headed—that exhilarating finish in and with God—he could put up with anything along the way: Cross, shame, whatever. And now he's there, in the place of honor, right alongside God. When you find yourselves flagging in your faith, go over that story again, item by item, that long litany of hostility he plowed through. That will shoot adrenaline into your souls!

Jesus took the sin of the world upon himself so that we could obtain the prize of eternal life. The ESV Study Bible reminds us, "The cross of Christ represents the greatest suffering in History, for Jesus not only suffered physically but also experienced God's wrath in taking upon himself the sin of the world."[10]

Jesus paid the ultimate sacrifice so that you and I *can* overcome the trials of this world. Let's keep our eyes fixed on Jesus, knowing the saints are cheering us on to victory. Choose to run this race of life with abandon, knowing that there is an eternal reward for those who persevere.

Declarations

Do not be overcome by evil; overcome evil with good.

Jesus paid the ultimate sacrifice so that you and I *can* overcome the trials of this world.

Overcoming in Your Life

How has your belief in Jesus and His sacrifice on the cross inspired you to be an overcomer? Detail a specific instance and explain what it has meant to you in your life.

_____
_____
_____
_____
_____
_____
_____

If you are struggling to fight the good fight of faith today, ask Jesus to help you overcome.

_____
_____
_____
_____
_____

DAY 5

The sin in our lives that we fail to conquer will eventually conquer us. —Warren Wiersbe[11]

As Christians, we must be continually on guard. We have a target on our backs and the enemy has us in his crosshairs. We should be quick to identify sin in our life and confess it right away.

In *Overcoming the World: Grace to Win the Daily Battle*, Joel R. Beeke says,

> "The Path to gain is through pain. The Christian life is a struggle, it demands entrance through a narrow gate and a daily walk along a narrow path. The Christian way is not a middle way between extremes but a narrow way between precipices."[12]

Read Matthew 7:13-14: "Enter by the narrow gate. For the gate is wide and the way is easy that leads to destruction, and those who enter by it are many. For the gate is narrow and the way is hard that leads to life, and those who find it are few."

According to Matthew 7:13-14, what gate should we enter?

_____

_____

What else do we learn about the narrow gate?

_____

_____

What do we learn about the wide gate? Where does it lead?

_____

_____

The way to eternal life is narrow because it is only through Jesus Christ that we may gain entrance. There is no other way—not through the universe, Buddha, Allah, or any other man, woman, or way. Jesus is the way. He is the narrow gate. Salvation comes by grace alone, through faith alone, in Christ alone. Once we make our way through the narrow gate, we should remain on the narrow path.

Sit, Walk, Stand

Watchman Nee, also known as Ni Tuosheng, was an influential Christian teacher and church leader who worked in China during the 20th century. He studied the word of God and believed that it was truly God's divine revelation to man. Nee did not have a seminary degree; however, he wrote several books that expounded on the Bible.

In his book *Sit, Walk, Stand*, Watchman Nee uses these three words to describe the Christian life. Nee reminds us that "God has done everything in Christ," and that we should "see ourselves as 'seated' in Christ."[13]

Our power comes from a resurrected, glorified Jesus. As we proceed on the narrow way, we too are seated with Christ in the heavenly realms. We can exercise victory once we understand our position in Christ. Because of the victorious power available to us through a resurrected Jesus, we can stand in faith against all that this world brings against us.

Not only can we simply stand, but we can be more than conquerors through Christ.

Read Romans 8:31-39:

> What then shall we say to these things? If God is for us, who can be against us? He who did not spare his own Son but gave him up for us all, how will he not also with him graciously give us all things? Who shall bring any charge against God's elect? It is God who justifies. Who is to condemn? Christ Jesus is the one who died—more than that, who was raised—who is at the right hand of God, who indeed is interceding for us. Who shall separate us from the love of Christ? Shall tribulation, or distress, or persecution, or famine, or nakedness, or danger, or sword? As it is written, "For your sake we are being killed all the day long; we are regarded as sheep to be slaughtered." No, in all these things we are more than conquerors through him who loved us. For I am sure that neither death nor life, nor angels nor rulers, nor things present nor things to come, nor powers, nor height nor depth, nor anything else in all creation, will be able to separate us from the love of God in Christ Jesus our Lord.

We are more than conquerors in this life because of what Jesus Christ has done for us! Aren't you thankful that, as a child of God, you belong to Him? Because you belong to him and are greatly loved, nothing can separate you from his love! Nothing in my past can separate me from God's love, and nothing I do or don't do today can separate me from God's love. The same is true for you, my friend: Nothing in your past, present, or future can separate you from God's love. God's ultimate expression of love came to us through Christ's sacrifice on the cross of Calvary.

Jesus, the High Priest

According to Hebrews 4:14-16, Jesus is our Great High Priest. Read the passage in Hebrews and answer the following questions.

Where has Jesus passed through?

_____

_____

Because of this, what should we do?

_____

Jesus can sympathize with our frail humanity because he himself took on human form and was tempted yet remained without sin.

What does verse 16 tell us to do? What will we find there?

_____

_____

As Christians, we are to follow Jesus on the narrow path of life. We become more like Him as we spend time reading and studying the word and through prayer, practices that allow us to live victoriously and be more than conquerors.

Jesus knows our weakness and understands the temptations we face. When we put our faith and trust in Him, He lavishes His mercy and grace upon and makes us a new creation.

Our life on this earth is an opportunity for our loving creator to drawing us to Himself through His Son so that we can have a restored relationship with Him.

Declarations

God is for me and wants good for me.

Jesus is continually pleading my case before the Father in heaven.

I am more than a conqueror in Christ Jesus!

Nothing can separate me from the love of God.

Overcoming in Your Life

Take a moment to reflect on all that Jesus Christ has done for you through His death, burial, and resurrection. Praise and thank Him for the cross and that we can be made right with our heavenly Father.

_____
_____
_____

Week 5

COUNT IT ALL JOY WITH THE NEW TESTAMENT BELIEVERS

the rock

DAY 1

When you accept the fact that sometimes seasons are dry and times are hard and that God is in control of both, you will discover a sense of divine refuge, because the hope then is in God and not in yourself. –Chuck Swindoll[1]

Peter

As we continue to trace our theme of overcoming throughout the Bible, our study this week will focus on the New Testament. We will begin by focusing on Peter, also known as Simon Peter, and the first book of Peter. The book of Peter is a short book and contains only five chapters, but they are packed full of wisdom concerning persevering with hope through suffering.

Before we dig into the main text for today, let's look at a few verses about Peter and see what we can learn about him.

What do we learn about Peter in Matthew 14:29-31?

_____

_____

_____

In verse 29, we see Peter step out in faith to walk on the water, but in verse 30 he becomes afraid and cries out to the Lord. In verse 31, Jesus chastises him for not having faith.

Peter is the same disciple who later denies Jesus three times. Read Luke 22:54-62 to gain insight into Peter's denials.

What do we learn about Peter in Matthew 16:18?

_____

_____

What else do we learn about Peter in Matthew 16:21-23?

_____

_____

_____

Peter began to rebuke Jesus. What was Jesus's response in verse 23?

_____

_____

When Jesus appears to the disciples after the resurrection, he sits down and has breakfast with them. It is at that point that we learn something interesting.

Read John 21:15-17. What does Jesus tell Peter to do?

_____

_____

_____

The first thing that Jesus asks Peter is "do you love me more than these"?

Peter responds, "Yes, Lord; you know that I love you."

In John 21:15, Jesus tells Peter to "feed my lambs," and in John 21:16, Jesus says, "feed my sheep." Finally, in verse 17, He reminds Peter yet again: "Peter, if you love me, then feed my sheep." In John 21, Jesus asks Peter three times if he loves him and tells him that if he does, he should feed his sheep. (Remember that this is the very same Peter who was rebuked in Matthew 16:21-23.)

Now read Matthew 26:30-36.

What does Jesus say to Peter in verse 31?

_____

_____

What is Peter's response in verse 33?

_____

_____

What does Jesus tell Peter will happen in verse 34?

_____

_____

What is Peter's response?

_____

_____

Peter is an unlikely hero. Peter was a common, ordinary fisherman, but he was chosen as one of the original twelve disciples that followed Jesus. He was the one who walked on water but began to sink when doubts assailed him. Although he professed love for Jesus, he also denied Him three times. At one point, Jesus rebuked him and said, "Get behind me, Satan!" Yet Jesus said that the church would be built upon Peter and that, if Peter loved Jesus, he would feed the lambs of God. You see, God calls and uses men and women despite their ability. He knows our frail human condition and still chooses to ask us to take part in His kingdom work.

Keep everything we learned about Peter in mind and read 1 Peter 1:1-12.

Peter wrote his letter to encourage the early New Testament believers who were confused by the persecution they were suffering.

What do we learn about salvation in 1 Peter 1:3-5?

_____

_____

_____

What do we learn about trials in verses 6-9?

_____

_____

_____

What do we learn about our inheritance?

_____

_____

_____

Now read 1 Peter 1:13-21.

How does it say we should live in verses 13-16?

_____

_____

Where does our faith and hope come from, according to verse 21?

_____

_____

Peter encourages believers to stand strong and remember all that Christ has done through his resurrection. Those who place their faith and trust in Jesus Christ receive a glorious, incorruptible inheritance. Through these verses, Peter encourages believers to trust in the Lord and promotes a life of obedience, regardless of circumstances.

Declarations

Through Jesus, I am born again to a living hope.

I have an imperishable, undefiled, and unfading inheritance that is kept in heaven for me.

I will not conform to my former passions of ignorance but will be holy as Jesus is holy.

Overcoming in Your Life

Do you ever feel like you can't be used by God for sins that you committed in the past or things that you are doing in the present?

_____

_____

_____

God's love is greater than our sin. He chooses the foolish things of the world to confound the wise. Jesus loves you and wants to restore you. He has called you to specific works that only you can do!

What is He saying to you today?

_____

_____

_____

DAY 2

I believe in the sun even if it isn't shining. I believe in love even when I am alone. I believe in God even when he is silent." —Found on a cellar wall in Cologne, Germany, where Jews hid during World War II[2]

When following Jesus, will you remain a faithful witness to Him, even if life doesn't go as planned? Will you have faith to believe even when your circumstances don't add up?

Today we will turn our study to the book of Acts. This book records the early church movement and the spread of the gospel after the resurrection of Jesus.

What do we learn about the spread of the gospel in Acts 1:8?

_____

After they were filled with the Holy Spirit, Christians were called to be witnesses of the gospel message and spread the good news throughout the world. The word "witnesses" in Greek is μάρτυρες, *martyres*, which is where we get the word martyr.[3] I don't know about you, but I don't associate the word "witness" with the potential for death. However, according to the *Oxford English Dictionary*, a martyr is "a person who is killed because of religious or other beliefs."[4]

Stephen

We are going to spend our time today looking at Stephen, the first ultimate witness for Jesus Christ. Begin by reading Acts 6:1-7.

In verse 5 we meet Stephen. He is referred to as a man full of faith and the Holy Spirit. He was chosen as a man devoted to prayer and the ministry of the word.

I love what verse 7 says: "And the word of God continued to increase, and the number of the disciples multiplied greatly in Jerusalem, and a great many of the priests became obedient to the faith." Our modern-day church was established by a few individuals who were obedient and faithful to God. We never know what He will accomplish through us and our obedience to Him.

Stephen was preaching to the diaspora Jews. These were Jews who were living outside of Palestine.

In Acts 6:8-15, we read about the arrest of Stephen. Read the passage to see what else we can learn about his story.

What does verse 8 tell us about Stephen?

_____

_____

What more do we learn in verse 10?

_____

_____

What was he accused of in verses 11 and 13?

_____

Stephen was full of the Spirit and spoke with wisdom. In verse 14, he was most likely referring to what Jesus said in Mark 14:58 about destroying the temple and rebuilding it in three days. He was charged with blasphemy, accused of speaking against Moses (the Law) and against God.

Look up Mark 14:63-64 and note what Jesus was accused of in these verses.

_____

_____

Now go to Matthew 26:59-60 and note the similarities between the trial of Jesus and the trial of Stephen.

_____

_____

What did Jesus predict would happen to his followers in John 15:18-21?

_____

How does Acts 6:15 describe Stephen?

_____

_____

Read Exodus 34:29-30 and Matthew 17:2 and note the similarities between Stephen, Moses, and Jesus.

_____

_____

Stephen recounts a brief history of the Old Testament to the Sanhedrin in Acts 7:1-53. The Sanhedrin was the religious council of the day, made up of the High Priests and Elders. They were considered to be the supreme religious leaders. Stephen concluded his speech by turning the accusation of his accusers in Acts 7:51-53.

What accusation did Stephen make?

_____

_____

Stephen continued to share his vision of the exalted Christ and, in doing so, made the high priests angry. Let's wrap up today's lesson by reading about this in Acts 7:54-8:3.

Acts 7:54 tells us that the high priests were enraged with Stephen, but what do we learn about Stephen in verse 55?

_____

_____

Stephen was filled with the Holy Spirit and, in that moment, saw the glory of God and Christ seated at his right hand. We see the high priests' anger intensify toward Stephen.

How did the Sanhedrin respond in verses 57 and 58?

_____

_____

Stephen remained faithful to Jesus Christ until the very end. In verse 59 he cried out to God as he was being stoned. Right before he died he prayed, "Lord, do not hold this sin against them."

Stephen died praying for the very men who killed him. His final prayers were "Lord Jesus, receive my Spirit," and "Lord, do not hold this sin against them."

Saul Ravages the Church

In Acts 8:1-3, we learn that Stephen's death was approved by Saul and triggered a period of intense persecution for the church. Acts 8:2 explains, "And there arose on that day a great persecution against the church in Jerusalem." In addition, "Saul was ravaging the church, and entering house after house, he dragged off men and women and committed them to prison."

We will learn more about Saul and his transformation from persecutor to overcomer tomorrow, but until then let's close by thanking God for Stephen. Stephen's life and death was a powerful example to us. May we learn from his example and be found faithful, holding on to Jesus Christ until the end!

Declarations

Strengthen me to be a faithful witness, Lord.

I will remain faithful to Jesus Christ until the very end!

Overcoming in Your Life

What does remaining faithful in today's world mean to you? What attitudes and behaviors characterize that faithfulness?

_____

_____

_____

_____

Will you choose to remain faithful, even if it means making uncomfortable choices?

_____

_____

_____

Spend some time in prayer, thanking God for Stephen's example to us.

_____

_____

_____

Finally, let's conclude today's lesson with the hope-filled words of the final stanza of "Be Thou My Vision."

"High King of heaven, my victory won
May I reach heaven's joys, O bright heav'n's sun
Heart of my own heart, whate'er befall
Still be my vision, O ruler of all"[5]

God can use anyone

DAY 3

The blood of the martyrs is the seed of the church. —Tertullian[6]

Saul/Paul

God can use anyone, even the most unlikeliest of characters. Today we will study the man who went from persecuting the church to becoming one the biggest champions of spreading the gospel: Saul, who is also known as Paul. (Saul is his Jewish name, and Paulous or Paul is his Greek name.)

Yesterday, we read Romans 8:1-3 and learned that Saul was persecuting the church until he had an encounter with the Lord. We pick up today by reading about Saul's conversion in Acts 9.

The Conversion of Saul

Read Acts 9:1-22.

What does verse 1 say Saul was doing?

_____

_____

While on the road to Damascus, looking for Christians to arrest, Paul encounters Jesus. What happens in verse 3?

_____

_____

When Paul encounters a light from heaven, he hears a voice. What does he hear in verse 4?

_____

_____

When Jesus asks Saul why he is persecuting Him, Saul questions Him in return. In verse 5, he asks, "Who are you, Lord?" What response does he hear in verse 5, and what is he told to do in verse 6?

_____

_____

_____

In these verses, we see Saul (or, as we will refer to him in the remainder of this lesson, Paul) intensely persecuting Christians. He does so until he has an encounter with the living God, Jesus Christ.

In verse 11, Jesus tells Ananias to go look for Paul and help him regain his sight. Ananias is confused. He questions the Lord in verse 13, saying, "Lord, I have heard from many about this man, how much evil he has done to your saints at Jerusalem."
How does the Lord respond in verse 15?

_____

_____

At one point or another in our lives, we are all like Paul. We may not actively persecute the church but, until we meet Christ, we are all on a path that leads to destruction. Once we encounter the living God and see our great need for Jesus, we are in a position to have a conversion experience. Like Paul, we are never the same again.

God's Chosen Instrument

Paul was God's chosen instrument to spread the gospel to the gentiles and proclaim the name of Jesus to both kings and the children of Israel. Paul's life experiences uniquely qualified him to spread the gospel. Sometimes the circumstances of our life don't appear to make sense, but if we surrender our lives and yield to the Lord, we too can make a difference for the kingdom.

Let's look at some other scriptures that will give us clues to as why Paul was uniquely qualified as God's chosen instrument.

What do we learn about Paul in the following verses?

Romans 11:1

_____

_____

Acts 22:3

_____

_____

Acts 26:4

_____

_____

Acts 23:6

_____

_____

Acts 16:7

_____

_____

Paul was a descendant of Abraham from the tribe of Benjamin. Born in Tarsus and educated by the preeminent teacher Gamaliel, Paul was not only of Jewish descent, he was also a Pharisee and Roman citizen. Paul's past experiences equipped him to be able to speak to Roman leaders, Jews, and Gentiles alike. He knew the law and the Torah but also understood the fulfillment of the law, Jesus Christ.

Created for a Purpose

Man's chief end is to glorify God, and enjoy Him forever. —Westminster Shorter Catechism[7]

Everything that happened in Paul's life served a purpose in his calling. Do you know that you have been created for a purpose? Each of us are fearfully and wonderfully created in the image of Almighty God, positioned on this earth to fulfill the good works He has divinely appointed. You were uniquely created to live in this particular time period in history. No matter who you are, God has work for you to do!

Our salvation is not based on works. There is nothing we can do to save ourselves. We will never be good enough, work hard enough, or be enough. We are saved in Christ alone! However, the more we seek to be like Jesus and become more conformed to his image, the more we will *want* to become like him. Our experience with salvation fills us with the desire to tell others about Him and share His great love. Our gratitude for Christ's sacrifice spurs our desire to serve others and advance the kingdom.

Declarations

Everything changed when I had encounter with the living God, Jesus Christ.

Jesus redeemed me from my past mistakes. I have been washed clean.

He has chosen to use me for His glory and He calls me for a specific purpose.

Overcoming in Your Life

Friend, sometimes we can feel unworthy of the call of Jesus on our lives. We carry the weight of sin, guilt, or shame from past mistakes and it stops us from being all that we are called to be in Christ. I am sure that Paul, who ravaged the church and persecuted Christians, didn't feel worthy of his call. However, that didn't stop him from spreading the gospel and advancing the kingdom of God.

If you feel unworthy of your calling, confess those feelings to the Lord now, laying the weight of your sin and shame at the foot of the cross.

_____
_____
_____

Is there something from your past that uniquely qualifies you to testify to a particular group of people? Perhaps it is somewhere you have lived or something you have done. What clues do you see in your past that uniquely qualify you?

_____
_____
_____

Ask God to show you something specific from your past that has equipped you for your future works, praying that He will show you what He wants you to do.

_____
_____
_____

Praise Him that you are fearfully and wonderfully made for a purpose. God has blessed you with unique gifts and talents, coupled with an extraordinary perspective on the world based on your life experiences.

DAY 4

To be a Christian is to seek to do the will of God at all costs. Yet it often happens that the harder we try, the more we feel cramped by failure. We must have help, or give up in defeat. In short, we must be "saved by faith" if we are to act in faith. –Georgia Harkness[8]

All of the overcomers we have studied up to this point have been men. However, there are several examples of women who overcame sin, adversity, rejection, and other challenges in both the Old and New Testaments.

Let's close out this week by looking at a few overcoming women from the New Testament.

The Syrophoenician Woman

We find the story of the Syrophoenician woman, a gentile, in Mark 7:24-30 and Matthew 15:21-28.

Begin today's lesson by reading both of these accounts.

What did this woman want?

_____

_____

What was the initial response of Jesus?

_____

_____

How did she respond?

_____

_____

What was the outcome?

_____

_____

Jesus was trying to escape the crowds when this woman followed him, begging and pleading with him to help her daughter. She was desperate for her daughter's healing, which caused her to be bold and persistent.

How often today are we desperate to hear from Jesus?

_____

_____

Are we persistent in our prayers to Jesus when they go unanswered?

_____

_____

What about when He tells us no? Do we return to Him and continue to beg for healing?

_____

_____

We all have the common problem of sin, but what differentiates us is what we do with it. Are we going to be like the Syrophoenician woman and be persistent in our prayers, or would we rather stay stuck in our sin?

When we faithfully follow the Lord with obedience, we are delivered from sin.

The Chronically Ill Woman

We read the account of a woman with an issue of blood in several books of the Bible. Read the following passages from Matthew 9:20-22, Mark 5:25-34, and Luke 8:43-48.

How long did the woman hemorrhage?

_____

What made her well?

_____

What additional details do we learn from reading Mark 5:25-34?

_____

_____

_____

The account of this woman is listed in the three aforementioned gospels, but we are never told her name. However, there is much to be learned from this nameless woman. Can you imagine the exhaustion she must have felt from the continuous bleeding she experienced—something that made her culturally "unclean"—for twelve years? She suffered at the hands of many physicians, but because of her faith, she was instantly healed. When she touched the hem of Jesus's garment, He immediately knew that someone had touched Him because He felt power leave Him. Because of her faith and her bold action, she was instantly healed.

The Samaritan Woman at the Well

Jesus loved women and treated them with respect. We read the encounter between Jesus and another unnamed woman, simply referred to as the Samaritan woman, in John 4. Conclude today's study by reading John 4:1-30.

What does Jesus say to the woman in verse 7?

_____

The woman was shocked that Jesus, a Jew, asked her for a drink. It was not customary at the time for Jewish men to speak to women in public, especially when the man was Jewish and the woman was Samaritan. The Jews despised the Samaritan people. Even the disciples were amazed to see Jesus speaking with the women at the well.

What does Jesus say to her in verse 10?

_____

How does Jesus follow up His response in verses 13 and 14?

_____

_____

At that point, the woman asks Jesus for the living water He has told her about and leaves the well to tell others in her city what she has experienced. In that moment, the Samaritan woman was transformed and began sharing her good news.

What makes the Samaritan woman's transformation even more amazing is that, during the encounter, Jesus confronted the woman about her past sins. He knew all of the sins she had committed, just as He knows all of our sins. Yet He chose to use her and He chooses to use us, despite our past mistakes. When we put our faith and trust in Jesus and repent of our sins, He can use us to accomplish great and mighty works for the kingdom.

Declarations

I will boldly and consistently pray and seek answers to my prayers.

God loves me and forgives me. He washes me clean and gives me eternal life.

Overcoming in Your Life

Which of the women studied today do you identify with most? Why?

_____

_____

Do you have a prayer request that has gone unanswered by the Lord?

_____

_____

If so, have you continued to wait on the Lord for an answer or have you given up?

_____

_____

Do you pursue unanswered prayers? If not, what is holding you back?

_____

_____

Do you have the courage to pursue Jesus with the same boldness of faith of that these New Testament women pursued Him?

_____

_____

DAY 5

O Father . . . I bless Thee for counting me worthy of this day and hour, that in the number of the martyrs I may partake of Christ's cup, to the resurrection of eternal life of both soul and body in the imperishability that is the gift of the Holy Ghost. –Polycarp[9]

Polycarp is considered to be one of the foundational martyrs of the church. Yet, even as he walked to a brutal execution, he praised and thanked God for his goodness, demonstrating joy in the face of death.

This attitude—choosing to praise God in the midst of the storm—is the focus of our time together today.

Struggles of a Young Mom

Being a mom of young children is not for the faint of heart. Mountains of laundry, diapers, and constant messes day after day are a challenge. Motherhood teaches you a lot about yourself and your character, for better or for worse. By the time I became pregnant with my youngest, I already had two sons at home and had just recovered from a cornual uterine ectopic pregnancy that nearly took my life. I already had an active eight-year-old that I was homeschooling and a special needs toddler who suffered from many medical issues and required constant care. My busy life was challenged even more when I was required to go on bed rest for my entire pregnancy. To complicate matters, we lived next door to my husband's parents, who were both diagnosed with brain tumors. We battled weariness, illness, grief, and loss, and we struggled to make sense of what God was doing in our lives during those difficult years.

The book of James became my lifeline during those difficult years. James is filled with practical wisdom to apply to daily living. It also has a lot to say about our struggles and what we should do when trials arise.

Lessons from James

We will conclude this week's study with a look at James, the brother of Jesus, who was known as James the Just. The book of James tells us how to live out our faith.

As James describes, God allows tests and trials to come into our life. These trials help us to become spiritually mature. Look up the following verses and see what James teaches us about trials in James 1:2-12.

In James 1:2-4, what do we learn about trials?

_____

What does it say about man in James 1:12?

_____

_____

What can we learn about our crown in 1 Corinthians 9:25?

_____

_____

God wants us to *count it all joy* when we experience trials, because it is those trials that test and perfect our faith so that we are complete. If we don't know what to do, we are to ask for wisdom, something God generously provides. We ask for wisdom in faith, knowing that God wants to answer our prayer.

James 1:2-5 from The Message Bible further illuminates the text:

> Consider it a sheer gift, friends, when tests and challenges come at you from all sides. You know that under pressure, your faith-life is forced into the open and shows its true colors. So don't try to get out of anything prematurely. Let it do its work so you become mature and well-developed, not deficient in any way. If you don't know what you're doing, pray to the Father. He loves to help. You'll get his help and won't be condescended to when you ask for it.

Now read James 1:13-18. What do we learn about temptation in verse 13?

_____

_____

Who tempts us, according to verse 14?

_____

_____

According to verse 17, from whom do we receive all good gifts?

_____

_____

God allows trials and tests to come into our life, but He is not the one who tempts us. We are lured away by our own evil desires and, when we don't check those desires, they lead us to sin. We are God's beloved children and He gives us good gifts.

Again, The Message Bible further illustrates verses 13-18:

> Don't let anyone under pressure to give in to evil say, "God is trying to trip me up." God is impervious to evil, and puts evil in no one's way. The temptation to give in to evil comes from us and only us. We have no one to blame but the leering, seducing flare-up of our own lust. Lust gets pregnant, and has a baby: sin! Sin grows up to adulthood, and becomes a real killer. So, my very dear friends, don't get thrown off course. Every desirable and beneficial gift comes out of heaven. The gifts are rivers of light cascading down from the Father of Light. There is nothing deceitful in God, nothing two-faced, nothing fickle. He brought us to life using the true word, showing us off as the crown of all his creatures.

We are not tempted by God; we are tempted by our own evil desires. That is why we must keep a short account of our sins, and make confession a regular practice. Through Jesus, our advocate, we have direct access to confess our sin to the Father. Jesus advocates continually on our behalf.

Read James 1:19-25.

What should everyone be quick to do?

_____

_____

What are we to put away?

_____

_____

What will save our souls?

_____

_____

What are we warned of in verse 22?

_____

_____

Finally, what do we learn from verse 25?

_____

_____

The crown for faithful perseverance is the promise of eternal life with all its abundant blessings. If we remain faithful until the end, we will receive a blessing. But as the verses clearly say, we must be doers of the word and not hearers only. Although trials will come in this life, they are designed to help us become spiritually mature. The person who endures and remains faithful to the end receives the crown of life. This is not an earthly crown or tiara encrusted with precious stones, it is the crown of eternal life.

Don't become weary in doing good; hold on, for we have an eternal reward!

Perseverance can be a challenge when troubles arise. James 5:13 tells us what we are to do when we suffer. If you suffer, what does James say to do?

_____

_____

What does 5:16 say we should do?

_____

_____

What a privilege it is to pray in faith and to pray for one another. The prayers of the righteous are powerful. We are to faithfully pray for the sick, the lost, and for one another. Our prayers make a tremendous difference, and we should never underestimate the power of prayer.

Declarations

I choose joy, despite the trials I face, because I know that the testing of my faith produces steadfastness and makes me a mature Christian.

I pray to God and believe that He is a good Father who hears my prayers and wants to give me good gifts.

I am quick to hear. I am slow to speak. I am slow to anger.

When suffering comes, I pray with hopeful expectation that the Lord will save me.

Overcoming in Your Life

Think of a time in your life when you experienced a trial and chose to count it all joy. What did you learn from that experience?

_____
_____
_____
_____

What would you say to a friend going through a difficult time to encourage him or her?

_____
_____

Sometimes, we have to preach to ourselves to remind ourselves of God's goodness and faithfulness in our life. Conclude this week's study by making a gratitude list of times in your life when God proved Himself faithful to you.

_____
_____
_____
_____
_____
_____

Week 6

REWARD FOR THE FAITHFUL

what must soon take place

DAY 1

Most of those facing persecution today could have escaped if they had denied their faith. The question is not whether we are persecuted, but whether we are willing to lay down our life in Jesus. —DC Talk[1]

Our journey of studying what it means to be an overcomer concludes in the final book of the Bible, the Revelation of Jesus Christ. We will examine the letters written to the seven churches in the book of Revelation to learn about the blessings awaiting those who overcome. These were seven actual churches that existed in Asia Minor. As we study them, we will also analyze the spiritual principles that are applicable to our lives today. In doing so, we will see that by faith, Christ helps us overcome. For those who succeed in standing firm to the end, there is a blessing awaiting them in heaven.

Blessings in My Life

The Lord has bestowed many blessings in my life, from an incredible husband and three wonderful boys to a nice home, cars to drive, and food to eat. These are wonderful, earthly blessings but I know that someday the stuff of this earth will rot away. Eventually, there will be a day of judgment when all things will pass away.

Along with the more obvious blessings I have received, there have also been blessings in disguise. The difficult trials I experienced were painful at the time, but looking back, I can see now that they were a blessing in my life. For example, when I broke both of my arms, it didn't feel like much of a blessing. However, the chain of events that occurred after my arms were broken brought me a greater sense of God's love, His peace, and His provision for my life and for those I love.

In Revelation, there are many rewards or blessings described for the overcomer. These are not earthly gifts like we have now; they are glorious, eternal, heavenly rewards. Before we receive these blessings, there are some events that must occur.

What Must Soon Take Place

Keep in mind that John wrote the book of Revelation to encourage first-century Christians who were experiencing great suffering and intense persecution. Throughout the book, John describes a vision he has received that provides a heavenly perspective of the future and of what will soon take place.

It is important to note that Revelation is apocalyptic literature and is the only book of prophecy in the New Testament. Many people think of Revelation as a riddle or a mystery to be deciphered, and oftentimes people look for hidden codes or messages within the chapters, but the word "revelation" means the exact opposite.

In its original format, the word "revelation" comes from the Greek word *apokalupsis*, (ἀποκάλυψις), and it means an unveiling, uncovering, or revealing. The ESV Study Bible notes tells us that the literary genre is one of prophecy and contains a series of visions, but also incorporates elements of poetry, including imagery, metaphors, similes, and allusion. It goes on to say, "The most important thing to know about the literary form of the book of Revelation is that it uses the technique of symbolism from start to finish."[2]

As the ESV Study Bible notes, Revelation is full of symbolism. There are multiple ways to interpret the unfolding of events in Revelation. Scholars throughout the ages have debated the exact timeline for specific events. We will not address these myriad interpretations, as our purpose is simply to understand what the book says in regard to becoming an overcomer.

The Revelation of Jesus Christ

Let's examine the first letter to the seven churches to see what is revealed or uncovered.

Read Revelation 1:1-3. Who is this revelation about?

_____

_____

Where did this revelation come from?

_____

_____

When are these things going to take place?

_____

_____

What does it call the person who reads aloud the words of this prophecy, a person who hears and keeps what is written?

_____

_____

What do we learn about time in verse 3?

_____

_____

We learn that God gave John the Revelation of Jesus Christ through an angel, a messenger from God, to show the first-century Christians the things that would soon take place. God promised a special blessing in Revelation 1:3 to those who read the prophecy aloud and those who keep what is written. The time of Jesus's return is near and, as Christians, we should be watchfully waiting the return of our King Jesus.

When will these things happen? Again, we don't know the exact timing; we are only told the time is near.

The Number Seven

John greets the seven churches and writes a letter to each of them. You will see the number seven repeated throughout the book of Revelation. The number seven is often refers to completion.

Read Revelation 1:4-8.

What three things do we learn about Jesus Christ in verse 5?

1._____

2._____

3._____

What do we learn about Jesus in verse 7?

_____

_____

Jesus loves us. Through his precious blood, we are saved. We don't have to worry about missing His return; no one will miss it. Everyone will see Him, even the ones who persecuted Him. He is the beginning and the end, the great I am, who is, and was, and is to come. Hallelujah!

The Son of Man Among the Churches

In reading through Revelation, we see Jesus pictured among the seven churches. Let's close today's lesson with one final thought from the ESV Study Bible notes:

> Jesus Christ appears in resplendent and overpowering glory to reassure his churches that by his death and resurrection he has control of the danger and death that threaten them. Although He is exalted in Heaven, he is also present with his churches on earth and knows their needs better than they do themselves.[3]

Jesus is currently seated at the right hand of God but will one day return for his bride, the church. In the interim, although He resides in heaven, His Spirit remains with us on earth.

Declarations

There is a blessing for me if I read aloud the words of Revelation and keep what is written in it.

Jesus will one day return for His bride, the church.

The Lord understands the condition of my heart and knows exactly what I need.

Overcoming in Your Life

It is critical we understand our time on earth in conjunction with the kingdom calendar. When we understand that we are living in the last days, how should this knowledge impact the way we live our lives today?

_____
_____
_____
_____

Create a list of friends and family members who do not yet have a personal relationship with Jesus Christ. Then, spend some time praying over the list. Ask God to show you how you can best love them. Ask Him for wisdom on the best way to share your faith with them.

_____
_____
_____
_____

As followers of Jesus Christ, we have been given the greatest gift in the world! Our goal is to love God, love others, and tell as many people as we can about Jesus. Brainstorm ideas for stepping out of your comfort zone and sharing the hope that is within you with others. What might that look like for you in the coming days?

_____
_____
_____
_____

letters to the churches

DAY 2

If you feel and perceive such a faith in you, rejoice in it, and be diligent to maintain it, and keep it still in you; let it be daily increasing, and more and more be well working, and so shall you be sure that you shall please God by this faith; and at the length, so shall you, when his will is, come to him, and receive "the end and final reward of your faith," as St. Peter (1 Peter 1:9) nameth it...
—Thomas Cranmer[4]

The Church of Ephesus

We have so much to learn about being an overcomer in the book of Revelation. Let's begin by examining the first of the seven letters. The churches are listed in an order that traces the route in which a courier would have delivered them.

Begin by reading the letter to the church of Ephesus in Revelation 2:1-7.
Meditate on these verses and answer the following questions.

> To the angel of the church in Ephesus write: "The words of him who holds the seven stars in his right hand, who walks among the seven golden lampstands. I know your works, your toil and your patient endurance, and how you cannot bear with those who are evil, but have tested those who call themselves apostles and are not, and found them to be false. I know you are enduring patiently and bearing up for my name's sake, and you have not grown weary. But I have this against you, that you have abandoned the love you had at first. Remember therefore from where you have fallen; repent, and do the works you did at first. If not, I will come to you and remove your lampstand from its place, unless you repent. Yet this you have: you hate the works of the Nicolaitans, which I also hate. He who has an ear, let him hear what the Spirit says to the churches. To the one who conquers I will grant to eat of the tree of life, which is in the paradise of God."

What are the Ephesians commended for in verses 2 and 3?

_____

_____

What is abandoned or lost in verse 4?

_____

_____

The church of Ephesus had doctrine and duty but no devotion. Man looks at the outward appearance, but God sees right to the heart of things. He knows whether or not we are just going through the motions. God knew what The Righteous Brothers knew in 1965 when they sang the song, *You've Lost that Loving Feeling*. The church at Ephesus was loveless.

115

They weren't doing everything wrong—they were commended for patiently enduring, detesting what is evil, testing the spirits, and their ability to suss out false teachers.

What does verse 5 say to do in response to verse 4?

_____

_____

Verse 5 is packed full of goodness! The first thing it says to do is *remember* from where you have fallen. Don't forget the old life from which you have been saved. Then it says to *repent*. In other words, turn away from your wicked ways. Confess your sins. Remember how you felt when you first became a Christian. Do the things you did when you first became experienced a relationship with Christ. In addition, read your Bible, pray, and tell others what He has done in your life!

What does it say to the one who conquers or overcomes in verse 7?

_____

_____

Jesus says, *listen up—this is important!* Clean out your ears and open your heart to hear what the spirit is saying. For those who overcome will eat of the tree of life, which is in the midst of paradise with God. The one who remains faithfully devoted until the end to Jesus will gain the reward of eternal life. Gaining victory is the objective that sustains Christians as they face the trials and tribulations of spiritual warfare. The Lion of Judah, the root of David, the sacrificed lamb of God redeems the people of God through the crucified messiah, and it is his death that gives us eternal life.[5]

We fight our battles from a place of victory, knowing that Jesus Christ has conquered death, hell, and the grave. We have read the end of the book and know who wins. However, while we are here on earth, we will all experience difficulties. During those challenges, we must keep our eyes fixed on Jesus and let His great love and sacrifice remain in the forefront of our minds. We must remember our first love and continue to do the things we did when we first fell in love with Jesus. We will overcome!

The Church of Smyrna

Next, let's look at the letter written to the church in Smyrna. Begin by reading Revelation 2:8-11:

> And to the angel of the church in Smyrna write: "The words of the first and the last, who died and came to life.
>
> "I know your tribulation and your poverty (but you are rich) and the slander of those who say that they are Jews and are not, but are a synagogue of Satan. Do not fear what you are about to suffer. Behold, the devil is about to throw some of you into prison, that you may be tested, and for ten days you will have tribulation. Be faithful unto death, and I will give you the crown of life. He who has an ear, let him hear what the Spirit says to the churches. The one who conquers will not be hurt by the second death."

In verse 8 it says, "The words of the first and last, who died and came to life."

Who is this referring to?

_____

_____

It is Jesus. Jesus is aware of the church's condition, and in verse 9 responds by saying, "I know your tribulation and your poverty, (but you are rich)." The believers in Smyrna were physically poor but spiritually rich. They suffered persecution, yet they endured.

Jesus warns the church in these verses that we will suffer, but he also provides an assurance in verse 10. What is that assurance?

_____

_____

Remaining faithful in the midst of those around us who are marked by compromise and wickedness is what gives us our reward. Jesus calls on the church to conquer through their faith in Christ. If they do so, they will be rewarded and receive the blessed reward of the crown of life, which is eternal life. With Jesus Christ living in us, and the hope of glory he provides, we have the power we need to remain faithful and overcome sin.

Again, he says to listen and pay attention. We see the repeated phrase, "He who has an ear let him hear." If you overcome and remain faithful to Jesus, then you will not be hurt by the second death.

Friend, these verses offer us so much encouragement. Throughout history, everyone who is part of the church will experience suffering to one degree or another. Some will even be called to die for their faith. No matter what happens to us in this life, we can put our faith and trust in Jesus Christ. That faith is our key to victory.

We don't need to be afraid of what might happen to us. Jesus says not to fear anything. He calls on the church to remain faithful and to endure persecution.

Declarations

I am victorious because Jesus has conquered death, hell, and the grave.

If I am faithful until the end, I will receive the crown of life.

Overcoming in Your Life

Think back to when you first heard about Jesus. Do you remember the zeal you felt? Are you still passionate for God, or are you simply going through the motions?

_____
_____
_____
_____
_____
_____

How do we keep our focus and love directed toward God when everything around us pulls us away from Him? Share your thoughts.

_____
_____
_____
_____

Have you lost your first love? If so, repent of your sin and turn to back to Jesus Christ.

_____
_____
_____
_____
_____
_____

Pray with me: _Lord, help us never to forget our first love. Without you, Jesus, we are hopeless. Thank you, Lord, for your plan of salvation. We are humbled by your great love and are grateful that you first loved us! Give us strength to endure the trials we face. May our love for you and others never grow cold. In Jesus's name, Amen._

the church of pergamum

DAY 3

Father, perfect my trust! Let my spirit feel, in death, That her feet are firmly set On the Rock of living faith! — Phoebe Cary[6]

Let's take a look at the next letter, sent to the church of Pergamum.

Believers in Pergamum faced false teaching and endured persecution. We read about how the church of Pergamum compromised in Revelation 2:12-17.

What complaint does Jesus have against this church?

_____

_____

The doctrine of Balaam refers to a prophet described in Numbers 22 in the Old Testament. Balaam was a false prophet who attempted to prophesy against the children of Israel and corrupt them through idolatry and immorality.

Let's see what else we can learn about Balaam in the following New Testament verses.

2 Peter 2:15

_____

_____

_____

_____

Jude 1:11

_____

_____

Return back to our verses in Revelation 2.

What does verse 16 say the church should do?

_____

_____

What are the consequences if they don't repent?

_____

_____

Now look up Matthew 6:24. What does it say?

_____

_____

Compromise has no place in the life of a Christian. You cannot serve the world and serve God!

Now take a look back at Revelation 2:17.

What two things are given to the one who conquers in verse 17?

     1._____

     2._____

What is written on the stone?

_____

_____

The hidden manna and the white stone with the new name on it are blessings or rewards for the faithful. According to the ESV Study Bible, "Historically, a white stone was given to victors at games for entrance to banquets; such a stone was also used by jurors at trials to vote for acquittal."[7]

Church of Thyatira

Moving through the letters to the churches, today we will focus on the letter to church of Thyatira. Before we do, let's go to Acts 16:11-15.
We meet Lydia in this passage. Where was she from?

_____

_____

What does this passage tell us about her?

_____

_____

Now that we've established those facts, let's return to our passage for today. We read more about this corrupt, morally compromised church in Revelation 2:18-29.

What does verse 19 tell us about this church?

_____

_____

What does the Lord condemn in verse 20?

_____

_____

The church in Thyatira was growing in their love, faith, patience and good works, yet they let false teaching and seductive spirits creep into the church, specifically the spirit of Jezebel. These churchgoers were unrepentant and continued to practice sexual immorality.

The Lord gave the false prophetess time to repent of her fornication, but she refused.
In verse 23, we learn how the Lord searches the hearts and intentions of people and gives to everyone according to their works.

Go to 1 Corinthians 11:31-32. What do we learn about judgment in these verses ?

_____

_____

An important part of our Christian walk is to take stock of our actions and keep our account short with the Lord and with others. We must be quick to forgive, to confess our sins, and to repent of our wrongdoing. The Lord disciplines us so that we won't be condemned along with the world.

In Revelation 2, we see that not everyone in the assembly was unfaithful. To those who remained faithful, the Lord encouraged them to hold fast in verse 25.

When we get to verse 26, we see another one of the rewards promised to believers.

What are the rewards for the overcomer as noted in verses 26-28?

_____

_____

Don't miss the oft-repeated phrase "he who has an ear, let him hear what the Spirit says to the churches." Any repeated phrase in the Bible is notable because it is repeated for emphasis. This phrase, in particular, is used as a warning to heed what is being said. We also see the repeated theme of remaining faithful until the end.

I love the way Matthew Henry concludes the commentary of Revelation 2:19:

> How tender Christ is of His faithful servants! He lays nothing upon his servants but what is for their good. There is a promise of ample reward to the persevering, victorious believer, also knowledge and wisdom, suitable to their power and dominion. Christ brings day with him into the soul, the light of grace and of glory, in the presence and enjoyment of Him their Lord and Savior. After every victory let us follow up our advantage against the enemy, that we may overcome and keep the works of Christ to the end.[8]

The Lord sees through our intentions and motives to our hearts. When we stray away from the good path, He lovingly disciplines us for our good. His desire is for us to live in victory! When we don't know what to do, we aren't left alone. He freely gives us wisdom, knowledge, and the power we need to live victoriously.

Church of Sardis

We read about the Church of Sardis in Revelation 3:1-6:

> And to the angel of the church in Sardis write: "The words of him who has the seven spirits of God and the seven stars.
>
> "I know your works. You have the reputation of being alive, but you are dead. Wake up, and strengthen what remains and is about to die, for I have not found your works complete in the sight of my God. Remember, then, what you received and heard. Keep it, and repent. If you will not wake up, I will come like a thief, and you will not know at what hour I will come against you. Yet you have still a few names in Sardis, people who have not soiled their garments, and they will walk with me in white, for they are worthy. The one who conquers will be clothed thus in white garments, and I will never blot his name out of the book of life. I will confess his name before my Father and before his angels. He who has an ear, let him hear what the Spirit says to the churches."

Why is the church of Sardis rebuked in Revelation 3:1?

_____

_____

What is the church told to do in verses 2 and 3?

_____

_____

What is the hope for the church in verse 4?

_____

_____

What promise is made to overcomers in verse 5?

_____

_____

Again we see the repeated verse concluding this section of scripture: **He who has an ear, let him hear what the Spirit says to the churches.**

On the surface, the church in Sardis looks alive, but it is rebuked for its dead works. The church's saving grace is a few members who remain loyal and pure and are considered worthy to walk with Jesus. The members of this church are told to remember what the word says, to hold on to it, and to repent of their sin. They are warned that Jesus will return like a thief in the night. Yet to the one who overcomes, there is the promise that they will be clothed in a white garment, that their name will never be blotted out of the book of life, and that it will be confessed before God and the angels.

Many American churches today look like the church in Sardis. The churches look alive, but they may be filled with people who need to repent of their sins and turn back to Almighty God. Church attendees and members who come to church each week simply to check a box, but don't live out their faith daily, are spiritually dead. Jesus sees our hearts and knows who is faithful and who is not.

The ESV Study Bible notes for Revelation 3:4-5 give us a clearer picture of this idea:

> Hope for revival is in the fact that **a few names**—alert and unstained disciples—can still be found in this church. Their unsoiled **garments** symbolize consistent obedience and courageous faith. Christ promises them the conqueror's reward: communion with Himself (**walk with me**) and the **white** raiment of victory. Their **name** is secure in His **book of Life**, and He will confess their **name** before the Father, since they have confessed Jesus in hostile circumstances.[9]

Let us learn from the church of Sardis to hold fast to the word of God, repent of our sins, and return to good works. If we do these things, we will have a great reward awaiting us in eternity.

Declarations

I will have an ear to hear what is being said to me through scripture.

I will keep the words of the Lord in my heart.

I will be on guard against false teaching.

I repent of my sin and proclaim Jesus as Lord.

Overcoming in Your Life

Many of our Christian brothers and sisters across the world face persecution today. There are many countries in the world where people aren't free to worship Jesus Christ or spread the gospel. We don't see that same kind of persecution in the United States, but that doesn't mean it will never happen. We must resolve in our hearts to remain faithful, like Daniel was in the court of Nebuchadnezzar, even if everyone around us compromises their beliefs. Don't look to your right or to your left to see what others may be doing; instead, keep your eyes fixed on Jesus.

What are some ways you see people compromising their beliefs today?
_____
_____

How would you encourage a brother or sister to remain faithful and not give in to compromise? What would you say?
_____
_____

Do you see any signs of persecution against Christians in America today?
_____
_____

What are some ways you could encourage your brothers and sisters in Christ across the world that are being persecuted for their faith?
_____
_____

As believers, we know that we will face persecution and be pressured by the world to compromise our belief in God. But the lesson we learned from the churches we studied today is that there are blessings for those who remain faithful.

Stay faithful, my friend, stay faithful!

the church of philadelphia

DAY 4

Today, we will look at what Jesus says to the sixth and seventh churches.

First, we read about the church of Philadelphia in Revelation 3:7-13:

> And to the angel of the church in Philadelphia write: "The words of the holy one, the true one, who has the key of David, who opens and no one will shut, who shuts and no one opens. I know your works. Behold, I have set before you an open door, which no one is able to shut. I know that you have but little power, and yet you have kept my word and have not denied my name. Behold, I will make those of the synagogue of Satan who say that they are Jews and are not, but lie—behold, I will make them come and bow down before your feet, and they will learn that I have loved you. Because you have kept my word about patient endurance, I will keep you from the hour of trial that is coming on the whole world, to try those who dwell on the earth. I am coming soon. Hold fast what you have, so that no one may seize your crown. The one who conquers, I will make him a pillar in the temple of my God. Never shall he go out of it, and I will write on him the name of my God, and the name of the city of my God, the new Jerusalem, which comes down from my God out of heaven, and my own new name. He who has an ear, let him hear what the Spirit says to the churches."

Jesus is referred to in these verses as the holy, true one who has the key of David. Jesus opens doors that no one can shut and shuts doors that no one can open.

Write out Isaiah 22:22.

_____

_____

Glance back at Revelation 3 and answer the following questions.

What is the church commended for and what are they promised in verse 10?

_____

_____

What is the warning given in verse 11?

_____

_____

What is the promise for conquerors in verse 12?

_____

_____

The people in Philadelphia patiently persevered through trial and tribulation. They kept God's word and didn't deny His name. Because of their faithfulness, Jesus promised to keep them from the hour of trial that is coming on the earth. They will be kept safe from the wrath of God that will be poured out onto the world.

The ESV Study Bible's note on Revelation 3:10 illuminates this verse:

> To those who **have kept** his word, Christ promises, "**I will keep you**" from the coming **hour of trial**, which will put **those who dwell on the earth** to the test. Because this trial is **coming on the whole world**, it seems that before the final consummation , Revelation envisions a brief period of intensified persecution for the church and of escalating manifestations of God's wrath against "those who dwell on the earth" a phrase designating a rebellious humanity. Jesus does not promise to spare believers from suffering or martyrdom but to shield them from his wrath and to transform martyrdom into triumph.[10]

The overcomers in Philadelphia are promised to be made pillars in God's temple. They will participate in the new Jerusalem and will have God's name written on them.
What does it mean to be a pillar in God's temple? Let's look at a few other New Testament scriptures for clues as to what this may mean. Write out the following scriptures.

Galatians 2:9

_____
_____

1 Corinthians 3:16-17

_____
_____

2 Corinthians 6:16

_____
_____

Now read 1 Peter 2:4-10:

> As you come to him, a living stone rejected by men but in the sight of God chosen and precious, you yourselves like living stones are being built up as a spiritual house, to be a holy priesthood, to offer spiritual sacrifices acceptable to God through Jesus Christ.
>
> For it stands in Scripture:
>
> "Behold, I am laying in Zion a stone, a cornerstone chosen and precious, and whoever believes in him will not be put to shame." So the honor is for you who believe, but for those who do not believe, "The stone that the builders rejected has become the cornerstone," and "A stone of stumbling, and a rock of offense." They stumble because they disobey the word, as they were destined to do.
>
> But you are a chosen race, a royal priesthood, a holy nation, a people for his own possession, that you may proclaim the excellencies of him who called you out of darkness into his marvelous light. Once you were not a people, but now you are God's people; once you had not received mercy, but now you have received mercy.

We learn that James, Cephas, and John are referred to as pillars. As Christians, we ourselves house the temple of the living God, as His spirit dwells in us. He is our God. We are His people, members of the household of God, and believers who are part of His divine family. Jesus Christ is the cornerstone of God's temple, and through Him, we are made into a dwelling place for God by the Holy Spirit.

Church of Laodicea

Our final church is the church of Laodicea. We read about the lukewarm church of Laodicea in Revelation 3:14-22:

> And to the angel of the church in Laodicea write: "The words of the Amen, the faithful and true witness, the beginning of God's creation.
>
> "I know your works: you are neither cold nor hot. Would that you were either cold or hot! So, because you are lukewarm, and neither hot nor cold, I will spit you out of my mouth. For you say, I am rich, I have prospered, and I need nothing, not realizing that you are wretched, pitiable, poor, blind, and naked. I counsel you to buy from me gold refined by fire, so that you may be rich, and white garments so that you may clothe yourself and the shame of your nakedness may not be seen, and salve to anoint your eyes, so that you may see. Those whom I love, I reprove and discipline, so be zealous and repent. Behold, I stand at the door and knock. If anyone hears my voice and opens the door, I will come in to him and eat with him, and he with me. The one who conquers, I will grant him to sit with me on my throne, as I also conquered and sat down with my Father on his throne. He who has an ear, let him hear what the Spirit says to the churches."

Notice how Jesus does not commend this church for anything. It is the only church that does not receive a commendation. Instead, the message to this church begins with condemnation.

What do we learn about this church in Revelation 3:15?

_____

What is the consequence of this in verse 16?

_____

What do we learn about the church's true condition in verse 17?

_____

What are they instructed to do in verse 19?

_____

Write out verse 20 in the space below.

_____
_____
_____
_____

What is the reward to the overcomer in verse 22?

_____
_____

The church of Laodicea had become self-reliant and apathetic towards Christ. Deceived by their wealth, they were ambivalent to spiritual things and thus blinded to their depravity. Jesus wants communion with His church, and because of this, He calls us to repentance. Like the Laodiceans, our material wealth will only satisfy us temporarily and can blind us to what we need the most. Only Jesus can truly satisfy the longing of our souls.

Declarations

I will patiently persevere through trial and tribulation.

Jesus, help me to remain faithful until Your return.

As an overcomer, I will one day share in Christ's future kingdom.

Overcoming in Your Life

What is Jesus saying to you through today's study of the churches of Philadelphia and Laodicea?

_____

_____

In light of what we read today, examine your spiritual condition.

_____

_____

Praise Jesus! He loves us so much and has great rewards for those who overcome!

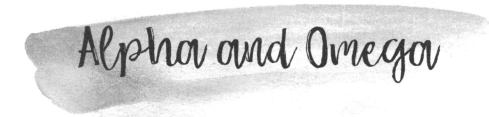

Alpha and Omega

DAY 5

I am the Alpha and the Omega, the first and the last, the beginning and the end. –Revelation 22:13

We have reached our final day of study! Today we will conclude with some beautiful truths from Revelation. We have a glorious inheritance awaiting us in heaven, and one day we will see our Lord and Savior face-to-face.

The Throne in Heaven

After the letters to the churches in Revelation, John is given a glimpse of the throne in heaven. Read Revelation 4:1-11.

What captures your attention in these verses?

_____

_____

What a beautiful glimpse we are offered in these verses as to the majestic brilliance awaiting us in heaven. We cannot even fathom the glory that awaits us in heaven. I love the words Bart Millard penned to the song, *I Can Only Imagine*, which sparks our imagination as to what it may be like when we get to heaven.

What do you think heaven will be like? How do you think you will respond when you get there? These things are fun things to ponder. Let's see what else we can learn from Revelation.

The Scroll and the Lamb

Read Revelation 5.
Why can we rejoice based on Revelation 5:5?

_____

_____

What is said of Jesus in verse 12?

_____

_____

Jesus is the lion of the tribe of Judah, the root of Jesse, and the promised conqueror of the Old Testament. He is the lamb that was slain, and only He is worthy to be honored, worshipped, and praised.

Write out Revelation 17:4.

_____
_____
_____
_____

In Revelation 19, there is rejoicing in heaven, and we read about the marriage supper of the Lamb. What does Revelation 19:9 say?

_____
_____

Chapter 19 concludes with the rider on the white horse. Read Revelation 19:11-16:

> Then I saw heaven opened, and behold, a white horse! The one sitting on it is called Faithful and True, and in righteousness he judges and makes war. His eyes are like a flame of fire, and on his head are many diadems, and he has a name written that no one knows but himself. He is clothed in a robe dipped in blood, and the name by which he is called is The word of God. And the armies of heaven, arrayed in fine linen, white and pure, were following him on white horses. From his mouth comes a sharp sword with which to strike down the nations, and he will rule them with a rod of iron. He will tread the winepress of the fury of the wrath of God the Almighty. On his robe and on his thigh he has a name written, King of kings and Lord of lords.

Who is the rider on the white horse and how is he described?

_____
_____
_____
_____

A victorious Jesus Christ defeats the dragon, the beast, and the false prophet. Satan is defeated in Revelation 20 and we learn of the great white throne of judgment:

> Then I saw a great white throne and him who was seated on it. From his presence earth and sky fled away, and no place was found for them. And I saw the dead, great and small, standing before the throne, and books were opened. Then another book was opened, which is the book of life. And the dead were judged by what was written in the books, according to what they had done. And the sea gave up the dead who were in it, Death and Hades gave up the dead who were in them, and they were judged, each one of them, according to what they had done. Then Death and Hades were thrown into the lake of fire. This is the second death, the lake of fire. And if anyone's name was not found written in the book of life, he was thrown into the lake of fire.

Jesus Christ will one day return victorious. He will defeat Satan and judge the people of the earth. On that day, every knee will bow and every tongue will confess that Jesus Christ is Lord of all. The destruction of the enemy will usher in a new heaven and a new earth.

Get Ready, Jesus is Coming

Let's close our study with these words from Revelation 22:6-20:

> And he said to me, "These words are trustworthy and true. And the Lord, the God of the spirits of the prophets, has sent his angel to show his servants what must soon take place."

"And behold, I am coming soon. Blessed is the one who keeps the words of the prophecy of this book."

I, John, am the one who heard and saw these things. And when I heard and saw them, I fell down to worship at the feet of the angel who showed them to me, but he said to me, "You must not do that! I am a fellow servant with you and your brothers the prophets, and with those who keep the words of this book. Worship God."

And he said to me, "Do not seal up the words of the prophecy of this book, for the time is near. Let the evildoer still do evil, and the filthy still be filthy, and the righteous still do right, and the holy still be holy."

"Behold, I am coming soon, bringing my recompense with me, to repay each one for what he has done. I am the Alpha and the Omega, the first and the last, the beginning and the end."

Blessed are those who wash their robes, so that they may have the right to the tree of life and that they may enter the city by the gates. Outside are the dogs and sorcerers and the sexually immoral and murderers and idolaters, and everyone who loves and practices falsehood.

"I, Jesus, have sent my angel to testify to you about these things for the churches. I am the root and the descendant of David, the bright morning star."

The Spirit and the Bride say, "Come." And let the one who hears say, "Come." And let the one who is thirsty come; let the one who desires take the water of life without price.

I warn everyone who hears the words of the prophecy of this book: if anyone adds to them, God will add to him the plagues described in this book, 19 and if anyone takes away from the words of the book of this prophecy, God will take away his share in the tree of life and in the holy city, which are described in this book.

He who testifies to these things says, "Surely I am coming soon." Amen. Come, Lord Jesus! The grace of the Lord Jesus be with all. Amen.

What is the blessing in Revelation 22:7?

_____
_____

We are left with one final warning in verse 19. What does it say?

_____
_____

Revelation 20 concludes with the words, "Surely I am coming soon." Jesus will one day return to judge the living and the dead. On that day, every knee will bow and every tongue will confess that Jesus is Lord.

Declarations

Lord, I praise You. You alone are worthy to receive glory and honor and power!

Come, Lord Jesus, come.

Overcoming in Your Life

Are you living your life with the thought of Jesus's eventual return in mind?

_____

_____

If you knew Jesus was returning today, what would you do differently?

_____

_____

Throughout this study, we have learned what it means to be an overcomer. We have explored the character qualities of the overcomer and seen them demonstrated as faith, integrity, steadfastness, and perseverance. The Bible contains everything we need know in order to live a victorious life. My prayer for you as we close is that you will fall further in love with Jesus and His word. I pray that you will continue to study so that one day you will hear the words,

"Well done, my good and faithful servant."

"He will wipe away every tear from their eyes, and death shall be no more, neither shall there be mourning, nor crying, nor pain anymore, for the former things have passed away."

~ Revelation 21:4

Promises to Overcomers

Will eat from the tree of life. - Revelation 2:7

Will not be hurt by the second death. - Revelation 2:11

Will be given a white stone. - Revelation 2:17

Will reign with Christ on His throne. - Revelation 2:26-27, 3:21

Will be given the morning star. - Revelation 2:28

Will be clothed in bright garments. - Revelation 3:5

Name will be in the book of life. - Revelation 3:5

Will be made a pillar in God's temple. - Revelation 3:12

Will participate in the new Jerusalem. - Revelation 3:12

Will have God's name written on them. - Revelation 3:12

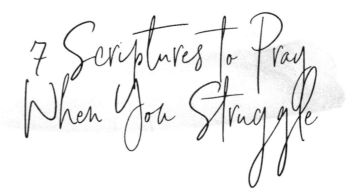

7 Scriptures to Pray When You Struggle

1. Trust in the Lord with all your heart, and do not lean on your own understanding. In all your ways acknowledge him, and he will make straight your paths. - Proverbs 3:5-6

2. So do not lose heart. Though our outer self is wasting away, our inner self is being renewed day by day. For this light momentary affliction is preparing for us an eternal weight of glory beyond all comparison, as we look not to the things that are seen but to the things that are unseen. For the things that are seen are transient, but the things that are unseen are eternal. -2 Corinthians 4:16-18

3. God is our refuge and strength, a very present help in trouble. - Psalm 46:1

4. Have I not commanded you? Be strong and courageous. Do not be frightened, and do not be dismayed, for the Lord your God is with you wherever you go. - Joshua 1:9

5. Seek the Lord while he may be found; call upon him while he is near. - Isaiah 55:6

6. And my God will supply every need of yours according to his riches in glory in Christ Jesus. - Philippians 4:19

7. No temptation has overtaken you that is not common to man. God is faithful, and he will not let you be tempted beyond your ability, but with the temptation he will also provide the way of escape, that you may be able to endure it. - 1 Corinthian 10:13

About the Author

Misty Phillip is an author, speaker, podcaster, mastermind leader and Bible teacher who is passionate about helping inspire women through the challenges of life. She encourages women to seek Jesus, study God's Word and grow in grace. Misty has overcome many trials and tragedies in her life with the help of God and uses her life experience to equip women to trust God through the struggles of life.

When she is not working, you will find Misty spending time with her husband, boys, and friends. Misty is head over heels in love with Jesus and loves geeking out in God's word. Hospitality is her passion; she loves to cook and fill her farm table with family and friends.

As mastermind leader Misty gathers women in her home each month to encourage women in their callings Kingdom work. Misty is the founder and host of the By His Grace Podcast sought after speaker, blogger and podcast guest. Misty is a contributor at A Wife Like Me and collaborator on the Dear Wife book.

Website
If you enjoyed The Struggle is Real: But So is God Bible Study and would like some free resources and more information go to **MistyPhillip.com**

Social Media
Connect with Misty for more inspiration, and encouragement.
Blog: MistyPhillip.com
Facebook: Misty Phillip
Instagram: @MistyPhillip
Twitter: @MistyPhillip
Pinterest: Misty Phillip
LinkedIn: Misty Phillip

Endnotes

WEEK 1

1. Edmund Clowney, *The Message of 1 Peter* (Downers Grove, IL.: InterVarsity Press, 1989).

2. "Overcome," *Cambridge Dictionary*, Cambridge University Press, accessed 18 December 2018, http://www.dictionary.cambridge.org.

3. "Overcome," *Merriam-Webster Online Dictionary*, Merriam-Webster, Inc., accessed 18 December 2018, http://www.merriam-webster.com.

4. "3528: Nikeo." *Strong's Concordance*, Bible Hub, accessed 18 December 2018, http://www.biblehub.com.

5. Kenneth Wuest, *Wuest's Word Studies From the Greek New Testament: For the English Reader Volume 1* (Grand Rapids, MI: Wm B. Eerdmans Publishing Company, 1955): 149.

6. Craig Koester, *Revelation: A New Translation with Introduction and Commentary* (New Haven, CT: Yale University Press, 2014).

7. Helen Keller, *Optimism: An Essay* (New York, NY: T.Y. Crowell and Company, 1903).

8. Adam Clarke, *Adam Clarke's Commentary on the Entire Bible* (Kansas City, MO: Beacon Hill Press, 1967).

9. Dwight L. Moody, *The Overcoming Life* (New York, NY: Fleming H. Revell Company, 1896).

10. "3533 Kabash." *Strong's Concordance*, Bible Hub, accessed 18 December 2018, http://www.biblehub.com.

11. "Pride," *Merriam-Webster Online Dictionary*, Merriam-Webster, Inc., accessed 15 March 2019, http://www.merriam-webster.com.

12. "Arrogance," *Merriam-Webster Online Dictionary*, Merriam-Webster, Inc., accessed 15 March 2019, http://www.merriam-webster.com.

13. "Rebellion," *Merriam-Webster Online Dictionary*, Merriam-Webster, Inc., accessed 15 March 2019, http://www.merriam-webster.com.

14. Catherine Marshall, *Christy* (New York, NY: Avon Books, HarperCollins Publishers, 1996).

15. Tony Evans, *Victory in Spiritual Warfare* (Eugene, OR: Harvest House Publishers, 2011).

16. Sun Tzu, *The Art of War* (Oxford: Clarendon Press, 1964).

17. S. M. Baugh, "Study Notes on Ephesians," *ESV Study Bible* (Wheaton, IL: Crossway Bibles, 2008): 2273.

18. Matthew Henry, *Matthew Henry's Commentary on the Whole Bible* (London: Fleming H. Revell Company, 1707).

WEEK 2

1. Jay E. Adams, "How to Overcome Evil: A Practical Exposition of Romans 12:14-21,"

(Phillipsburg, New Jersey: Presbyterian and Reformed Publishing Co. , 1977).

2. Charles Haddon Spurgeon, *Prayers from Metropolitan Pulpit: C. H. Spurgeon's Prayers* (Charlotte NC: Strait Gate Publications, 2009).

3. Wayne Grudeum, *Systematic Theology* (Grand Rapids, MI: Zondervan; Leicester: InterVarsity Press, 2000).

4. Ibid.

5. Erik Thoennes, "Biblical Doctrine: An Overview," *ESV Study Bible* (Wheaton, IL: Crossway Bibles, 2008): 2530.

6. Ibid..

7. Sun Tzu, *The Art of War* (Oxford: Clarendon Press, 1964).

8. "Beloved Stand: A Study in the Book of Jude." *Simply Scripture*, accessed 14 March 2019, https://www.simplyscripture.org.

9. Matthew Henry, *Matthew Henry's Commentary on the Whole Bible* (London: Fleming H. Revell Company, 1707).

10. Brennan Manning, *All is Grace: A Ragamuffin Memoir* (Colorado Springs, CO: David C Cook Publishers, 2011).

11. Joseph Benson, *Benson's Commentary—The New Testament* (New York, NY: T. Mason & G. Lane, 1839).

12. Matthew Henry, *Matthew Henry's Commentary on the Whole Bible* (London: Fleming H. Revell Company, 1707).

13. Jennifer Rothschild, *66 Ways God Loves You* (Nashville, TN: Thomas Nelson, 2016).

WEEK 3

1. C.S. Lewis, *The Weight of Glory* (New York, NY: HarperCollins, 2001).

2. Walter A. Elwell, *Baker's Evangelical Dictionary of Biblical Theology* (Grand Rapids, MI: Baker Book House Company, 1996).

3. Charles Marshall, *Shattering the Glass Slipper* (USA: M Power Resources, LLC, 2002).

4. John Bunyan, *The Pilgrim's Progress and Other Select Works of John Bunyan* (Green Forest, AR: Master Books, 2005): 771.

5. H.G. Wells, *The Wheels of Chance* (Norwood, MA: Norwood Press, 1905).

6. "Resolve," *Merriam-Webster Online Dictionary*, Merriam-Webster, Inc., accessed 18 December 2018, http://www.merriam-webster.com.

7. Bakht Singh, *The Overcomer's Secret: Studies in the Book of Daniel* (Bombay: F.C. Durham, 1972): 7.

8. Ibid.

WEEK 4

1. Augustine of Hippo, *Confessions*. Trans. by Henry Chadwick (Oxford: Oxford University Press, 2008): 3.

2. John MacArthur, *The MacArthur Bible Commentary* (Chicago, IL: Moody Publishers, 1999).

3. "Supreme," *Merriam-Webster Online Dictionary*, Merriam-Webster, Inc., accessed 18 December 2018, http://www.merriam-webster.com.

4. Robert Murray McCheyne, *The Works of the Late Rev. Robert Murray McCheyne, Vol. II* (New York, NY: Robert Carter, 1847): 53.

5. Dwight L. Moody, *The Overcoming Life* (New York, NY: Fleming H. Revell Company, 1896).

6. Chuck Swindoll, *Three Steps Forward, Two Steps Back* (Nashville, TN: Thomas Nelson, 1997).

7. Joseph Benson, *Benson's Commentary—The New Testament* (New York, NY: T. Mason & G. Lane, 1839).

8. Robert S. Candlish, *The First Epistle of John, Expounded in a Series of Lectures, Vol. 1* (Edinburgh: Adam and Charles Black, 1870).

9. Karen H. Jobes, *Zondervan Exegetical Commentary on the New Testament* (Grand Rapids, MI: Zondervan, 2014).

10. David W. Chapman, "Study notes on Hebrews," *ESV Study Bible* (Wheaton, IL: Crossway Bibles, 2008): 2383.

11. Warren W. Wiersbe, *Be Available* (Wheaton, IL: Victor Books, 1994): 18.

12. Joel R. Beeke, *Overcoming the World: Grace to Win the Daily Battle* (Phillipsburg, NJ: P&R Publishing Company, 2005).

13. Watchman Nee, *Sit, Walk, Stand* (Carol Stream, IL: Tyndale House Publishers, Inc, 1977): 5.

WEEK 5

1. Chuck Swindoll, "Thinking Theologically," *Insight for Living Ministries*, accessed 26 December 2018, www.insight.org/.

2. Max Lucado, "What Do You See?," *Max Lucado UpWords*, accessed 26 December 2018, www.maxlucado.com/.

3. "3144: Martus." *Strong's Concordance*, Bible Hub, accessed 14 March 2019, http://www.biblehub.com.

4. "Martyr," *Cambridge Dictionary*, Cambridge University Press, accessed 18 December 2018, http://www.dictionary.cambridge.org. https://en.oxforddictionaries.com/

5. Don Hustad, *Hymns for the Living Church* (Carol Stream, IL: Hope Publishing, 1981).

6. Tertullian of Carthage, *The Apology of Tertullian (Apologeticus)*, (Dalcassian Publishing, 2017).

7. Westminster General Assembly, *Westminster Shorter Catechism*, 1647.

8. Hugh T. Kerr, *Readings in Christian Thought* (Nashville, TN: Abingdon Press, 1990): 317.

9. Eusebius, *The History of the Church*, trans. by G. A. Williamson (London: Penguin Books, Ltd., 1989).

WEEK 6

1. DC Talk, *Jesus Freaks: Stories of Those Who Stood for Jesus: The Ultimate Jesus Freaks* (Tulsa, OK: Albury Publishing, 1999): 51.

2. Dennis E. Johnson, "Study Notes on Revelation," *ESV Study Bible* (Wheaton, IL: Crossway Bibles, 2008): 2464.

3. Ibid. 2466.

4. Hugh T. Kerr, *Readings in Christian Thought* (Nashville, TN: Abingdon Press, 1990): 174.

5. Dennis E. Johnson, "Study Notes on Revelation," *ESV Study Bible* (Wheaton, IL: Crossway Bibles, 2008): 2455.

6. William J. Bennett, *The Book of Virtues* (New York, NY: Simon & Schuster, 1993): 766.

7. Dennis E. Johnson, "Study Notes on Revelation," *ESV Study Bible* (Wheaton, IL: Crossway Bibles, 2008): 2465.

8. Matthew Henry, *Matthew Henry's Commentary on the Whole Bible* (London: Fleming H. Revell Company, 1707).

9. Dennis E. Johnson, "Study Notes on Revelation," *ESV Study Bible* (Wheaton, IL: Crossway Bibles, 2008): 2467.

10. Ibid. 2468.

Made in the USA
Monee, IL
03 March 2021